PopUp
REPUBLIC

PopUp
REPUBLIC

How to Start Your
Own Successful Pop-Up
Space, Shop, or Restaurant

JEREMY BARAS

WILEY

For general information on our other products and services or for technical support, please contact our Customer Care Department within the United States at (800) 762-2974, outside the United States at (317) 572-3993 or fax (317) 572-4002.

Wiley also publishes its books in a variety of electronic formats. Some content that appears in print may not be available in electronic books. For more information about Wiley products, visit our web site at www.wiley.com.

Library of Congress Cataloging-in-Publication Data:

ISBN-978-1-119-14591-2 (pb);
978-1-119-14747-3 (epdf);
978-1-119-14748-0 (epub)

Printed in the United States of America

10   9   8   7   6   5   4   3   2   1

Contents

Preface

QUITE OFTEN, A revolution takes place right before our eyes without our even being aware of it until it has already taken place. To understand why this occurs, think of a connect-the-dots drawing. The dots are all there in front of you, but until you connect them, you have trouble discerning what the picture actually portrays.

We are living in just such an era. The makeover is taking place in a confluence of four commercial sectors: retail; public dining; commercial and public property; and events. And it's happening because of a movement that is so new and fragmented that it doesn't have a definition, is spelled three different ways, even though it is only five letters, and its size depends on what you include within its umbrella, something that up to now is a matter of opinion.

The movement we are referring to is pop-ups, a/k/a pop ups, a/k/a popups. However you spell it, what can't be argued is that pop-ups are changing how artisans are making money; how commercial property owners are leasing their spaces; how big brands are launching new products; how celebrities are promoting themselves; and how e-tailers are marketing the merchandise they sell online.

And that is from the supply side. The convulsions are happening on the demand side as well. Consumers are now favoring locally made products, both for environmental reasons and because of a desire to know more about the merchandise they buy—where, how, and by whom a product was made. They want an antidote to the homogenization of choices that are offered by chain stores and chain restaurants. And while e-commerce offers convenience, it does that by eliminating the shopping *experience* that many shoppers feel is just as integral to the buying process as the items that are for sale. Pop-ups are the physical manifestations of popular trends (and trending hashtags) such as "Shop Local," "Small Business," and "D-I-Y."

The emergence of pop-ups is also being driven by economic factors. To borrow a phrase from the late Speaker of the House of Representatives, the Honorable Tip O'Neill, it's not only true that "All politics is local," but the same can be said for economics— all economics is local. Main streets, neighborhoods, communities, cities, regions, states—all have different problems and different elements that contribute to or detract from their financial well-being. Local economic development offices are tasked with providing the programs by which commerce should be strong and sustaining, but almost invariably, these offices have constrained budgets and few resources available to them. Pop-ups are proving to be vital tools—low-budget but highly effective—that are being used by economic development professionals to boost the local economies over which they have responsibility.

The objective of this book is to connect the dots. In Section 1, I aim to define what pop-ups are and, by virtue of that definition, what sub-sectors belong to the pop-up industry. With that accomplished, I attempt to determine the size of the industry, prevailing trends, who the key players are, and what factors are affecting its growth and direction.

In Section 2 I examine pop-ups in terms of how they relate to individuals—the opportunities they create for the merchant and the consumer as well as the venue owner. I attempt to answer the question: Are *you* a good candidate to launch a successful pop-up? And I explain how you can skew your odds toward that success.

In Section 3, all types of pop-up categories are analyzed, and I discuss how to execute various pop-up concepts.

In Section 4 I look at the future of pop-ups. The horizon is already coming into view as big brands and big malls look at the new omnichannel movement as the cutting-edge way that goods are marketed—a trend in which pop-ups have a major role to play. We are also putting forth a prediction—that when it comes to venues for pop-ups, there is a great, untapped potential for *personal residences* to serve as a primary source of spaces available for pop-ups.

Another intangible reason that pop-ups are becoming so pervasive is that they provide texture and discovery to what otherwise has become routine and even monotonous. Mention that you are going out to dinner at a restaurant around the corner, and it barely raises any eyebrows. But say you are going out to a pop-up restaurant around the corner, and everyone wants to know about it. Say that you are going shopping at the local supermarket and ask who wants to come, and you find that suddenly everyone is busy. But say that you are going shopping at a nearby farmers market, and suddenly you have to take the SUV to have enough room for everyone who wants to come along.

Pop-ups are quite frequently once-in-a-lifetime opportunities. They come, they go, and if you missed them, you probably won't be able to experience them ever again. But pop-ups also illustrate a great realization—that life is full of once-in-a-lifetime opportunities. So if you missed one pop-up, don't fret. Another one is likely to pop up next week!

Acknowledgments

THIS BOOK COULD not have been written without the help and guidance of a number of incredible individuals.

First, my family—my wife Marissa, my parents, Robyn and Larry Baras, my sisters, Samantha and Rachel, and, of course, (and arguably most importantly) my dog, Betty. You all have been tremendous sounding boards for me during this process, and the support that you have given to me throughout my career is immeasurable.

Special thanks go to Jeff Wang, Florence Hardy, Greg Spielberg, Aaron Gadiel, Laura Layton, Melinda Holland, Patty Hirt, and Shuchi Naidoo for being incredible interview subjects and for taking the time out of their busy schedules to answer a few questions. These folks are the best at what they do, and they are all doing great things for their respective industries.

My entire PopUp Republic team is phenomenal. Obviously, I wouldn't be in this position if it weren't for them. They have helped me build an outstanding company that is at the forefront of a growing, multi-billion-dollar industry, and I'm extremely grateful to work with them on a daily basis.

David Ghysels is an iconic figure when it comes to creating once-in-a-lifetime pop-up dining experiences. He is the founder of Dinner in the Sky (who also let me include some incredible photos!), an innovative dining experience that suspends patrons, via crane, over some of the most beautiful cities in the world.

I have great appreciation for the Community Entrepreneurship program at the University of Vermont, in particular Dr. Jane Kolodinsky and Dr. Chyi-Lyi (Kathleen) Liang. They are world-class professors at one of the premier schools in the country, and the Dollar Enterprise projected has singlehandedly helped form my entrepreneurial zeal.

Last, but not least, to every person who has been a client of PopUp Republic, organized a pop-up, attended a pop-up, or done something to help advance the industry, thank you. You are the reason why this book is written and what inspires me to do what I do every day.

Introduction

IN OCTOBER 2011, I had a reason to go to London and play tourist—my younger sister had started her junior year abroad at the London School of Economics, and I had some available vacation days coming from my job working for the Boston Red Sox. Although the job itself was rather low on the totem pole—I was a sales associate in the ticket office—it was nevertheless a dream come true and, as far as I was concerned, it was a stepping-stone toward a lengthy career in professional sports, my lifelong ambition.

My father tells of the time when he was talking to an old friend whom he hadn't seen in a while and, when the friend asked how his three kids were doing, my father replied, "Well, my oldest daughter is in Harvard Medical School, my youngest daughter attends the London School of Economics, and my son works for the Boston Red Sox."

"*Your son works for the Boston Red Sox!*" the friend exclaimed. He didn't care, nor did he probably even hear about what my sisters were doing. It was my association with the Red Sox that he found so incredible.

Anyway, my sister was engaged in her schoolwork, so one evening I sauntered over to The London Eye, the massive Ferris wheel that provides a birds eye view of the city. But as I neared the Eye,

I saw that it had been commandeered for some special event and that no tourists were being allowed to board.

The event?

Ticketed patrons (I found out later that tickets were about L15,000) were getting into the capsules for the trip around the hub, and as they circumnavigated, they were fed unbelievable courses by Michelin-starred chefs.

What I was watching was something I hadn't encountered before, certainly not in the United States—it was a pop-up restaurant!

It was one of the coolest things I had ever seen, and I started to look into it. Apparently, pop-up shops and pop-up restaurants were already the "in" thing in London, each one trying to outdo the other. But as my research continued, I saw that pop-ups were more than just clandestine, exclusive opportunities. They were also serious businesses, providing incremental income to brands, outlets for artisans, exposure to landlords, and tools for economic development offices to revive economically challenged high streets.

It immediately hit me that there both a problem and an opportunity were associated with pop-ups. The problem (it turned out there was more than one obstacle to overcome) was that there was no easy way for the public to find out about upcoming pop-ups, and few avenues through which merchants could promote them. This hit my entrepreneurial urges head on, and suddenly my job with the Red Sox didn't seem like such a stepping-stone after all. This was a service business I could embrace and about which I could be passionate, and I decided right then and there to start a business serving the pop-up industry in the United States, hoping to create a platform on which pop-up merchants and property owners could build a sustainable industry.

PopUp Republic was born when I returned to our shores, and there was no turning back.

■ ■ ■

Pop-ups are starting to become an accepted member of the mainstream economy. No matter where you live, it's not too difficult to find a pop-up shop, pop-up restaurant, supper club, or food truck in your neighborhood. In fact, when taking into account the market size of all of the categories that constitute a pop-up, including farmers and flea markets, yard sales, traditional pop-ups (shops, restaurants, and events), lemonade stands (yes, we consider those pop-ups as well), and food trucks, it reflects a sizable industry that measures between $45 and $50 billion, according to a study released by my company, PopUp Republic (which appears later in this book).

Additionally, cities like Oakland, New Orleans, Pittsburgh, Boston, and Detroit are all using pop-ups as a means to revitalize urban areas and spur economic growth in their communities. In some cases, local governments are even subsidizing the development and creation of pop-ups! Whether they're being used to launch a new product or draw incremental foot traffic, the increase in pop-ups over the last several years can be tied to several recent phenomena:

- **The "Buy Local" Movement:** Lately, there has been a large emphasis placed on locally made products. Customers like to know that the scarf they are buying is made by the person who is selling it—that it's not "Made in China" but instead is "Made Down the Street." By being made locally, not only is that scarf going to be cheaper, but it's also likely to be made with more care than one that is mass produced in a sweatshop on the other side of the world.
- **The "Fear of Missing Out":** In this day and age, people are continually striving for "bigger and better." Apple releases a new iPhone virtually every six months, and because it has a new feature that may or may not be useful, consumers often scramble to buy the newest, updated version, while the previous model, which may be just as functional, suddenly becomes obsolete. Similarly, if a pop-up opens in a vacant storefront, customers often flock to the shop before it's too late and they miss out on the product or service that is being offered.
- **The Economy:** In the economic crisis of 2008, the unemployment rate and the percentage of vacant storefronts on city streets increased dramatically. Because of this, the need of individuals to find creative ways to support their livelihoods

arose as much by necessity as opportunity. As a result, pop-ups became one of the solutions to all three of these issues. They created income-producing businesses and jobs, the former for those who organized them, the latter for the on-demand, temporary staffing that is usually needed to meet the influx of customers who attend pop-ups. Pop-ups have proven to be quite lucrative for landlords seeking to fill empty storefronts, providing commercial property owners with temporary rent, the ability to "stage" the venue while looking for permanent lessees, and, in some cases, turning temporary pop-up lessees into permanent tenants themselves. On top of all that, people are learning that they can make money from their hobbies, talents, and sheer ingenuity—many are finding that they can turn their hobbies and passions into new profitable businesses— a win for the merchant, a win for the landlord, and a win for the community!

The Pop-Up Industry

ONE OF THE newest innovations in retail is the *pop-up*—an ephemeral concept that provides customers with a "once-in-a-lifetime" experience. The industry has made tremendous strides over the last several years, especially in the United States, where brands both large and small are embracing pop-ups for a variety of purposes.

This section will dive into the deep world of pop-ups—from how and why they were started to the status of the industry today both domestically and abroad. We will touch on the nuances of the industry and the various categories within which they apply.

What Is a Pop-Up?

By DEFINITION, A pop-up is any event that is temporary and involves people taking part in it as hosts and attendees. As long as it has a given start and end date, it can be considered a pop-up. But as with just about everything in life, there are exceptions. For example, a driver's education course—while temporary in that it is likely to have a beginning and ending class—is not a pop-up, since it is an educational event that is only applicable to a certain demographic of individuals (those who are learning to drive). A lemonade stand, however, *is* a pop-up, since it is a business offering a product that is available to the public for a short period of time.

What constitutes a pop-up has a complex answer. In England, farmers markets are always considered sectors within the pop-up industry. In the United States, an explanation is needed as to why this was so in the U.K., and why it should likewise be deemed appropriate in the United States. The answer to the question "What is a pop-up?" probably can only truly be answered by the reply given by Supreme Court Justice Potter Stewart, who, when asked to describe what is meant by "hard-core pornography," replied that it was hard to define, "but I know it when I see it."

Using our stipulation that, whatever it is, its core element is that a pop-up is ephemeral, we have found ourselves debating the inclusion of food trucks. Are food trucks, which usually are at different locations at different times and can often appear at one-off food truck festivals, included in the definition of a pop-up? Or, because many are at the same location all year long, day in and day out, are food trucks excluded?

We decided that they are in, and for what we think is a very good reason. When we find ourselves explaining what we do and, specifically what a pop-up is, we give our fairly simplistic answer about it being a temporary shop or dining option. To which, as often as not, we would hear a response: "Oh yes! Like a food truck!" After hearing that enough times, we decided to let the public be the arbiter and to include food trucks among those sectors that fall under the pop-up canopy.

Once we defined, at least for our own edification, what a pop-up actually is, we had another question. How big was the industry? Was this a passing phase, or are temporary pop-ups, um, permanent? We had heard various numbers thrown around as to the size of the industry, but invariably, we discovered that each one referred to either too many retail and dining sectors as being part of the pop-up industry, or too few, so the market size they came up with was inherently erroneous. Not having a study to refer to, we decided to conduct one ourselves, and found a startling number: by best estimates, acknowledging that hard-and-fast empirical data were sometimes unavailable, it became clear that the monetary value of the pop-up industry was much higher than we thought—it is likely to be in the $45 to $50 billion dollar range, and perhaps a lot larger!

Another issue we confronted: Not only was a definition for the term "pop-up" needed and it was important to determine its size, but there wasn't even a consensus as to how to spell the five-letter word! Was it "pop-up?" Was it "pop up?" Or was it "popup?" We had seen all three spellings used. So we decided to check Google Analytics, and lo and behold, the preferred usage statistics were a dead heat between "pop-up" and "pop up." At least one spelling—"popup"—which happened to have been our preference, was eliminated!

Although not definitive, our sense is that "pop-up," with the hyphen, has emerged the victor, and that is the spelling we use for common, everyday reference. It still doesn't help us when we receive

Google Alert e-mails referring to articles that include allusions to pop-ups—we have to subscribe to Google Alerts for all three spellings to get a complete compendium, as even the almighty Google itself hasn't yet figured it out.

Even with such scrutiny and demarcations, the Google Alerts we receive also include the kinds of unwelcome pop-up advertisements that appear on web pages. No, we are not in that business, thank you. Nor are we involved in baseball, where pop-ups are one of the ways a hitter goes out. *Our* pop-ups are the good kind, and the kind that are re-inventing retail!

The Makings of
PopUp Republic

I'D LIKE TO begin this chapter by inviting you to skip it. In fact, although it is being slotted in as Chapter 2, it happens to have been the last chapter written for this book. It was practically an afterthought, even though, in retrospect, once written, I felt it was important enough to put toward the front.

The subject of this chapter is my own company, PopUp Republic. It isn't easy to justify devoting a chapter basically to writing about yourself, or at least about your own business, when you are tasked with writing the definitive, objective book about a subject matter about which readers might have an interest. But I'm doing it, and I think I not only have just cause, but it is actually an imperative if I am going to cover the topic of pop-ups, especially in the United States, in its entirety.

I say this for two reasons. First, "pop-ups" are a relatively new concept and industry. It represents the evolution of an amorphous group of disparate commercial trends into a growing, significant movement. While it can be illustrated that a so-called "pop-up" was hosted in the United States back in 1999 by a company named Vacant, and that this is justifiably referred to as the genesis of the pop-up industry in the United States, it was merely a foothold.

It is really only in the past three years or so that pop-ups have spread and become so popular that they have been embraced by big brands, artisanal creators, online retailers, commercial landlords, and celebrities as an indispensible marketing and commercial tour de force.

There have been three books written to date that we have heard of on the subject of pop-ups. *Pop-Up Retailer: How You Can Master This Global Marketing Phenomenon* was written by Christina Norsig, published in November 2011. Ms. Norsig has been referred to as "the queen of pop-ups" and can be considered an industry visionary, as evidenced by the date when her book was published—at the *beginning* of the launch of the American pop-up phenomenon. Her book came out just when the industry was starting to become what it is today.

Pop-Up Business for Dummies, published in paperback in December 2012, was written by London-based Dan Thompson and, while it alludes often to pop-ups in the United States, his Dummies book was more of a look at the pop-up scene in London and a reference for starting a pop-up business in the United Kingdom.

One of our favorite pop-up V.I.P.s in the U.S., Melissa Gonzalez, wrote the third book on pop-ups, *The Pop-Up Paradigm: How Brands Build Human Connections in a Digital Age*. This self-published 127-page guide came out in November 2014 and helps those who are thinking about launching a pop-up learn many of the issues that they should be considering.

But my book is the first attempt to capture the essence and direction of the pop-up industry as an already consequential participant in the rapidly changing retail culture of the United States. And to do that, we feel there is a requirement to establish before the reader both our bona fides and our street cred—street cred is important in the world of pop-ups, as most pop-ups are local, person-to-person, street-based enterprises (think of pop-up shops, food trucks, farmers markets, craft fairs, etc.).

The second reason I feel it is necessary to write about PopUp Republic is because it is the only end-to-end service provider to the pop-up industry. (We'll be explaining what we mean by that throughout this chapter.) As such, we have touched upon every aspect of the pop-up industry, and we continue to do this day in, day out, all over North America. Not a day goes by that we don't interact with pop-up chefs, pop-up merchants, pop-up vendors, big brands, pop-up landlords, and especially pop-up customers. We act as curators, marketers, advisors, espousers, and hand-holders.

For over three years, since the launch of PopUp Republic, we have been voracious studiers of the pop-up industry both here in the United States and around the globe. Around the clock, 24/7, our e-mail boxes are filled with Google Alerts, not only about "pop-ups," but on:

- Pop-ups
- Pop ups
- Popups
- Pop-up shops
- Pop up shops
- Popup shops
- Pop-up stores
- Pop up stores
- Popup stores
- Pop-up real estate
- Pop up real estate
- Popup real estate
- Pop-up hotels
- Pop up hotels
- Popup hotels
- Pop-up cafes
- Pop up cafes
- Popup cafes
- Pop-up restaurants
- Pop up restaurants
- Popup restaurants
- Supper clubs
- Supperclubs
- Food trucks
- Farmers Markets

Hundreds of Google Alerts fill our inboxes every day, and we try to read those that we feel are most relevant and important. In addition, we read such online resources as BuzzFeed, TechCrunch, *Fast Company*, The Consumerist, Business Insider, VentureBeat, Re/Code, Specialty Retail Report, American City Business Journals (and its local editions), Eater, Racked, Curbed, UpOut SF, *Miami Times*, UrbanDaddy, and a host of other online periodicals just to be sure we keep up with pop-up goings-on around the world, especially within the United States, and the marketing, dining, and retail trends that affect them.

Although we are still in the toddler stage, at least chronologically, we have already become the go-to resource for many media outlets. We've either been featured in or quoted by such venerable media sources as *TIME* magazine, *Forbes*, *CNBC*, *The Wall Street Journal*, *Independent Retailer*, and *VentureBeat*. When Fodor's wanted to print a special article on the top ten upcoming pop-ups across the United States, they turned to us to prepare the list. And when one of the world's leading publishers of business books and journals, John Wiley & Sons, was looking for an authority to write what it wanted to be the definitive book on pop-ups, they asked PopUp Republic.

What exactly made us be authorities? For one thing, our devotion to the pop-up industry falls somewhere on the bar graph between "passion" and "obsession." As of the writing of this chapter, we have pinned 5,578 pop-up-related photos on 144 boards on Pinterest. We have broadcast 11,641 tweets. We have published over 34,400 separate pop-up listings on our website's national pop-up directory. Looking for information on nearby farmers markets? Our directory lists over 1,000. In search of a special venue that accommodates pop-up events? Our listings surpass 1,200 traditional-to-eclectic opportunities.

But the answer as to why our own story is pertinent to understanding the pop-up movement in the United States actually lies deeper than what the numbers, however large, might imply. Rather, our story is told by the evolution of our business itself. Our business has expanded not only in terms of volume, but also in terms of breadth. As the industry kept changing and growing, so did the scope of our business as we tried to keep pace with the direction of the industry and its needs.

We started in 2012 with the goal of solving one major problem that confronted the industry as a whole and every single stakeholder in it—how to put the word out about upcoming pop-ups. That was the biggest issue facing the pop-up industry as we saw it.

Pop-up merchants had a great "product"—in short supply, in great demand, exclusive and exciting and eliciting that great fear-of-missing-out (FOMO) sense of urgency. In fact, as this trend continued to evoke excitement, many big brands started to append the word "pop-up" to one-off or short-term events they were sponsoring just to be associated with this new cutting-edge movement. "Pop-up" became a connotation, not just a genre.

But pop-ups had no clear way of promoting their businesses. No prior foot traffic. No prior word of mouth. No advertising budgets to speak of. Little to no marketing experience. No big, attractive buildouts. Often, not even a sign to hang on the door.

So PopUp Republic was launched to be a social media marketing company that focused solely on the pop-up industry. In particular, its specialty was in spreading the gospel about upcoming pop-up *events*, be they restaurants, shops, impromptu yoga classes, open artist studios, and others. Our hub was our website and its one-of-a-kind national directory, where pop-up impresarios could post their upcoming pop-up events, or we could do it for them. Pop-up listings, along with our blog posts, became our website's *content*.

Because pop-ups are not only so short-lived but, by their very nature, are usually impending within days or weeks, we chose Twitter as the primary social media supplement to our website. Twitter has an immediacy and reach matched by no other social media service we could find. We use Twitter to expound both about the pop-up universe at large as well as specific pop-ups that are listed on our directory, with the goals of helping to popularize the industry while at the same time driving consumer traffic to the pop-ups posted on our website. Because physical pop-ups are hyperlocal, looking to draw their audiences and shoppers from nearby areas, they don't have to reach millions. But they do have to publicize their event to a targeted group, either by category (foodies, fashionistas, etc.) or by location. This is the prime objective of our Twitter campaigns.

We chose to become active Pinterest participants as well. Pop-ups can be so cool, so unique, and so representative of the industriousness and ingenuity of their creators, that we wanted to portray this via pictures. They are also educational, and at times inspirational. When conducting Internet searches for pop-up events and topics, it is often our Pinterest images that appear at the top of the search results. If a picture tells a thousand words, then right now our Pinterest page is 5,578,000 words long!

Those three social media resources—our website, Twitter, and Pinterest—are the linchpins of our social media marketing efforts, abetted by periodic posts on Facebook and the issuance of press releases and public announcements.

But as time went on, we came upon other issues that were affecting the growth of the pop-up industry—not necessarily stunting its growth, but certainly not facilitating it either. The first related to venues.

Pop-Up Spaces is a two-sided issue, with two constituencies coming from two opposite directions with opposite needs—pop-up merchants and pop-up landlords.

Pop-up merchants are dependent on having a space in which to host their temporary events. The portfolio of spaces that would be suitable relates largely to the "vision" of the entrepreneur. Pop-up landlords have spaces that they would be willing to make available on a short-term basis to pop-up hosts.

The problem for the merchants was finding the proper venues, and the problem for the landlords was finding appropriate merchants. Although there existed commercial property companies and brokers, specialty leasing executives, and even a couple of new websites whose goal was to list spaces available for pop-ups, there was no efficient way for either constituency to find the other. This was becoming a big issue for the industry, as its fast-paced expansion and diversity of uses demanded an answer to this growing problem.

As a response, PopUp Republic developed a service by which pop-up merchants could find pop-up spaces, and vice versa. PopUp Republic uses similar social media resources as those it uses for promoting pop-up events. But by virtue of having three years of history with pop-up merchants through the listing of pop-up events, the company was also able to help match merchants with spaces in a more proactive way. PopUp Republic now counts over 1,000 pop-up-eligible spaces on its directory, with an additional 1,000 plus farmers markets at which booths are leased to merchants, usually on a seasonal or temporary basis.

Thus, our site provides solutions to two emerging needs by the pop-up industry: putting the word out about upcoming pop-ups and enabling prospective pop-up merchants and commercial properties to find one another.

But the industry kept growing, even in the three years since PopUp Republic was founded. Merchants needed more information, and they needed more help. To become more familiar with the ins and outs of merchants' and landlords' (and communities') requisites, we launched our own pop-up marketplace in Brookline, Massachusetts, working hand-in-hand with the property owner and town officials in what was more of a partnership than arms-length relationships. We all learned about what goes on in hosting a pop-up at the same time.

This information came in very handy not only in servicing small business pop-ups, but in helping the larger commercial properties capitalize on the emerging pop-up commercial opportunities. Whether because of the need for online retailers to have offline counterparts in the form of pop-ups, or because of their internally generated realization that they had large common areas that were not generating revenue—but could—major shopping malls undertook initiatives to play host to one-off pop-up events. The malls were facing competitive forces from many directions—online retail, farmers markets, the resurgence of urban commercial main streets, demographic shifts, and so forth—that led them to having to create means by which they could accommodate new realities. One solution they turned to was pop-ups, but again, they needed help in attracting and curating pop-up merchants and events. Again, PopUp Republic tweaked its own portfolio of services, providing assistance to the big malls in converting empty spaces into productive pop-up venues. These partnerships are now extending to big brand retailers, both online and offline, who recognize that pop-ups offer direct and personal access to their customer base, but are ill-equipped to respond to these opportunities.

As PopUp Republic recalibrated its breadth of services to coincide with the needs of pop-ups, it took on another initiative that provides a solution to a problem that the industry probably didn't realize it had. Not only was a pop-up shop in need of publicizing its upcoming opening, not only did it need a place to hold its short-term event, and not only were many of the participants in need of partnering assistance to have the event go off smoothly, but there was another obstacle that limited its growth. It was serving such a small target audience of shoppers. Even with the right marketing, the right location, and the right execution, they were being frequented only by a small number of nearby customers. Hyperlocal commerce has its pros and its cons.

But a lot was going on in the world of retail, many changes taking place as a result of technological advances. As new software and devices are developed and enhanced, we can expect these changes to continue, not necessarily in a straight line forward but by moving ahead, then backfilling where needed. This has become the case with online retailing. E-commerce continues to grow, but with that has come the realization of what new problems it is encountering along the way. One such problem is the need to provide a more personal shopping experience beyond the mere push of a button. Not only do shoppers want to see and sample products before they buy, but if they don't, they are more apt to return them to the purveyor, a costly matter for e-commerce suppliers. In order to overcome that problem, e-retailers have turned to offline stores—not permanent ones, with their huge commitments, but of the pop-up variety.

So the thought came to our minds—couldn't the reverse make sense as well? Couldn't those hyperlocal shops that are only open for short periods of time, that is, pop-ups, benefit by having the long reach of an online marketplace, one devoted exclusively to pop-up shops across the country? Why not take those ingredients that are most attractive to pop-up shoppers—supporting local small businesses, buying exclusive one-of-a-kind items, the fear of missing out on experiences—and extend the reach to shoppers around the country (actually, around the world)? You want to see what unusual items pop-ups in New York City have for sale today, but you are in Wichita, Kansas? That shouldn't be a problem in this day and age, so we launched a concurrent online marketplace for our listed pop-up shops to join, dubbed PopUps Across America.

As you can see, you can trace the evolution and expansion of pop-ups across America in recent years by following what PopUp Republic has morphed into as a response. What has emerged—both within the company and throughout the American pop-up scene—is just the beginning, an ecosystem in which an industry is being born and nurtured. As such, it enables the reader to gain a sense of what retailing has in store in the future. So excuse our insertion of this chapter, but it's probably true that what is going on within PopUp Republic is a microcosm of what is going on in the world of pop-ups.

Pop-Ups: The State of the Nation

IN THE UNITED states, pop-ups can be traced back to Colonial times and then throughout the ensuing centuries. Traveling salesmen went on road trips, stopping in town centers for several days to hawk their wares, then continued onward. Farm stands would spring up around harvest time, with farmers engaging in direct marketing to local consumers. Over the years, even children participated in the pop-up economy, setting up lemonade stands on street corners for a few hours on hot summer days.

But until fairly recently, pop-ups didn't really have a name, and there were no "pure" pop-ups as we know them today. In 1999, a company called Vacant in Los Angeles developed the concept for pop-up retail. The company began to sell limited edition items, and when the products sold out, it closed the store until a new shipment of items came in, at which time it would open again, albeit temporarily. The success of this concept led Vacant to shut its permanent store and instead open temporary shops at different target destinations. From there, one-off restaurants and supper clubs and one-off events have cropped up, slowly at first, but now at a rapid pace.

These days, pop-ups are practically ubiquitous—if you know where to look. The first "pop-up chef" of this generation is Ludo Lefebvre, the self-proclaimed "Impresario of Pop-Up Dining," who opened a roving secret dining concept in various locations throughout Los Angeles (he is also of *The Taste* fame, serving as a judge on the popular ABC reality cooking show). Target was one of the first major department store chains to open pop-ups within their stores, creating the opportunity for four smaller brands to appear in over 150 locations throughout North America in 2013. And Westfield, the ninth–largest shopping mall operator in the United States, launched Westfield Labs in 2012 as a means to create various experiential activation concepts to enhance the way brands connect with their customers, with pop-ups being an important part of this new strategy.

Today, thanks to Ludo, Target, Westfield, and other trendsetters, the pop-up industry in the United States is stronger than ever. In 2014, PopUp Republic had over 14,000 pop-ups listed on its site. This is just a fraction of what we estimate to be the total number of pop-ups that *actually* occurred in the United States during the same time period. Chefs are utilizing pop-ups as a means to test new menu items and experiment with new locations; makers are using them to create new monetization opportunities and to complement their existing online presence; large brands realize that customers need a "touch and feel" experience and are opening pop-ups to create a closer connection; and property owners need to find ways to drive incremental foot traffic and fill empty storefronts. All of these groups are finding that pop-ups are a great solution, which is why many people are convinced that the industry is not just a trend, but is the future of retail, public dining, and event entertainment.

Pop-Ups: The State of the World

POP-UPS ARE LIKE pretzels. Everyone claims that pretzels were first produced in their native country and can point to an exact time and place where that occurred. The fact of the matter is that pop-ups probably first appeared before history was even recorded. Itinerant merchants selling pelts, grain, and other wares would set up shop for a few hours or days in various towns along their routes. Farmers would sell their crops at harvest time from the side of the road. Before land was apportioned on the continent to the wealthy, which resulted in what we now call "jobs," most people had to fend for themselves, setting up businesses that often required them to be mobile and temporary rather than permanently located at one spot.

So pop-ups—as defined as being businesses or events that are temporary, requiring physical venues and physical shoppers, and having a start and end date—go back practically to the beginning of mankind's presence on earth. But in terms of recent history and modern-day commercial trends, we need to turn our attention to that place on the other side of the pond—the United Kingdom—and in particular to its capital, London, which arguably remains the pop-up capital of the world.

In London, pop-ups, especially in the form of pop-up shops, supper clubs, and farmers markets, comprise an important part of the retail and dining sectors of greater London and, to a somewhat lesser degree, the rest of the U.K. We can cite four examples of how advanced the pop-up industry is in England:

- In Camden, a district within London proper, pop-ups are so commonplace and integral to the economic well-being of the area that they are partially sponsored by the local municipality and are a line item in the annual budget.
- In London, Kerstin Rodgers, better known by her nom de plume Ms. Marmitelover, is credited with having launched the pop-up dining movement in the U.K. with her supper club, The Underground Restaurant. In 2010, she was named one of the 1,000 most influential people in London by *The Evening Standard*, and her blog is number 29 on the list of top blogs in the U.K. on any subject!
- Boxpark Shoreditch, located in the heart of East London, is a pop-up mall made up of shipping containers that has become a leading destination for indie fashion and lifestyle brands, cafes, and galleries of all sorts.
- Also noteworthy, although not conceived in London, is the international pop-up piano festival, Play Me, I'm Yours. Started in Birmingham, U.K., in 2008, fifteen pianos were situated across the city for three weeks for the public to play. All told, it is estimated that over 140,000 people either played or listened to the music from those pianos. Since then, the pop-up piano festival has gone international, reaching over six million people worldwide, with more than 1,300 pianos installed in parks, markets, train stations, and other unique settings in 46 cities across the globe.

Besides the U.K., the rest of Europe has begun to catch on to the pop-up phenomenon as well. One of the great bastions of the emerging pop-up movement, at least in terms of pop-up restaurants, is Helsinki, Finland. It is there that a group of friends founded what is called Restaurant Day in May 2011, an event that is now held around the world four times a year, in which thousands of people, in hundreds of cities, set up one-day pop-up restaurants, making Restaurant Day the largest food festival in the world.

In Paris, pop-up shops are beginning to compete with permanent stores, even the chic boutiques that line the main shopping districts in the city. But in addition to the pop-up retail stores, Paris can claim to be the original site of one of the world's premier pop-up dining events—Diner en Blanc.

Diner en Blanc is an exclusive secret outdoor dinner party that was founded over two decades ago by Francois Pasquier, with the first event held at the Bois de Boulange. Since then, it has spread to dozens of cities around the world—you can identify it from the attire of the participants, all of whom will be dressed up in white finery.

In Latin America, supper clubs are part of the culture. Known as "paladars," these dining events often have higher culinary standards than local restaurants. They offer the hosts the opportunity to set up a dining event without having to incur the costs and commitments inherent in permanent restaurants, and offer consumers an exciting dining scene that is at once high quality and often a little clandestine.

Although in most countries pop-ups have emerged as part of a trendsetting movement, there are some places where the pop-up industry came out of necessity. A series of devastating earthquakes in New Zealand was centered in the city of Christchurch and virtually destroyed its downtown shopping area. As a bridge to rebuilding the city, an effort that is expected to take decades, the community opted to build a pop-up marketplace, one that has become so popular that it is now counted as a "must see" destination for global tourists.

Pop-ups have clearly become an international movement, coming in all shapes and sizes—from Christmas marketplaces in Germany to impromptu restaurants in Poland, the Czech Republic, Australia, and elsewhere around the globe.

The Size of the Pop-Up Industry in the United States

A Case Study*

* *Author's Note:* PopUp Republic undertook a study in September 2014 to determine the size of the pop-up industry in the United States. Empirical data was lacking or somewhat dated for certain segments, hence a precise methodology and conclusive numbers were at times relegated to best estimates. The purpose of the study, though, was not to seek precision as to the industry's size, but rather to be able to wrap our arms around the magnitude of the industry for which we were looking to provide an ecosystem and to reach some consensus as to whether the pop-up industry was already a disruptive force in the retail, dining, and entertainment sectors—our conclusion is that there was no doubt that they were. Here is our report.

Profile of the Pop-Up Industry in the United States
Prepared by PopUp Republic
September 2014

PREVIEW

The pop-up industry is a fragmented market sector that nonetheless has emerged as a significant commercial force in the United States. There has never been a definitive study done of what constitutes "membership" in this category or how large the pop-up market is.

This industry report by PopUp Republic aims to establish a definition of what constitutes a "pop-up" and seeks to quantify just how large the market is. This latter objective will be represented by an informed estimate based on figures extrapolated from published sources.

DEFINITION OF WHAT CONSTITUTES A POP-UP

We have read write-ups that have sized the pop-up market in the United States to be anywhere from $8 to $80 billion. Neither of those numbers is accurate, as they either include or exclude commercial sectors that are or are not relevant. For example, many commentators have cited a 2012 Specialty Retail report as a source that estimated the size of the pop-up market to be $8 billion, but that estimate included kiosks and shopping mall carts and excluded other sectors that rightfully should have been included. Several other sources refer to the size of the pop-up market as being $80 billion, but differ as to whether this is relevant to the U.S. market or whether it is a worldwide figure. In referring to that number, some say it includes farmers markets, craft fairs, and pop-ups, while others say it includes clearance sales. And then there is a 2012 IBISWorld report, which indicated that there were 2,380 pop-ups in the United States in 2012, up from 2,043 the year before, with 68 percent being Halloween-themed. The conclusion one would reach from this calculation is that there were fewer than 800 non-Halloween pop-ups in the U.S. in all of 2012, which clearly means that farmers markets, flea markets, food trucks, yard sales, Christmas shopping market-places, and a host of other types of temporary retail sectors were excluded—in all likelihood, even pop-up dining events, since our anecdotal evidence from listings that were posted on our pop-up directory and our knowledge of the industry indicate there were far more than 800 pop-up restaurants and supper club dinners alone in 2012.

So then, what is a pop-up? It's time that this industry be defined.

The consensus is that a common feature of all pop-ups is that they are temporary. They can last an hour, they can last for months, but by definition, they have a beginning and an end. They don't necessarily have to be commercial, however. One of the original iterations of pop-ups was the flash mob, a musical or dance event in an unexpected pub-lic space that seemed to be spontaneous, although it was actually pre-planned. Today, a common example of non-commercial pop-ups are pop-up parklets—small, temporary, park-like settings that are established for public use in urban locations such as parking spaces. There are also pop-up exer-cise groups, walks, art exhibits, and many other examples of non-commercial pop-ups.

As part of the defined group, we elect *not* to include major events such as sports games and seasons, unless they are out of the ordinary or concerts or shows put on by famous celebrities, even though we acknowledge they too are temporary. It is a subtle distinction, but it goes along with the Supreme Court precedent of "We know it when we see it." But we do include events that are one-off community-oriented shows, festivals, or "happenings" (such as grub crawls, food/beer festivals, public poetry slams, and the like).

(*continued*)

(*continued*)

One note: We include food trucks as pop-up constituents, even though, admittedly, many are parked at the same location year-round, hence not exactly fitting the "temporary" qualification. We include the food truck sector as pop-ups for two reasons: First, many are temporarily located at a variety of locations, so even if they are open year-round, they may not necessarily be located at the same place year-round. Second, we often find that when trying to describe what pop-ups are to the unknowing, we provoke a response "oh, you mean like food trucks!" So part of the reason we include food trucks in the definition is because of public perception (this report isn't pretending to be completely empirical or scientific).

While not totally inclusive, our list of pop-ups includes the following:

- One-off or temporary dining events
- One-off or temporary retail shops/events
- Food trucks
- Farmers markets
- Flea markets
- Food/drink/entertainment festivals
- Yard/garage/estate sales
- Open artist studios
- Craft fairs

Again, there are others as well, but the above categories encapsulate the lion's share of pop-ups in the United States.

Size of the Pop-Up Market in the United States

Using the above definition and categories, we can better reach some valid, if somewhat estimated or projected conclusions about the size of the pop-up market in the United States. In calculating its size, we use as sources figures that have been generated either by the U.S. government, trade associations, or third-party research organizations.

Broken down by sub-category, we have found the following aggregated compilations:

Food trucks and street food vendors: According to a published report, this was a $1 billion market in 2013 and is projected to grow to $3 billion within five years. That said, we don't include street food vendors in our defined group, so we are estimating that the size of the food truck market in 2014 is about $1 billion, accounting for year-to-year growth of market, minus that allocated to street food vendors.

Farmers markets: The USDA estimated the size of the farmer-to-public market to be $7 billion in 2012. We have witnessed considerable growth in the number of farmers markets between then and the 2014 summer season and estimate that it is at least an $8 billion market currently.

Yard sales: Estimates we have read indicate that this is a $600 million to $1 billion market. Since the proceeds of yard sales go largely unreported, we elect to use the $1 billion as a conservative projection for 2014.

Flea markets: To our surprise, this comprises the largest segment of the pop-up market, with the industry's main trade association estimating that annual sales exceed $30 billion.

Others: This would include "pure" pop-up shops, restaurants, and supper clubs; food/drink/entertainment festivals; open artist studios; craft fairs; one-off classes; and other smaller segments that are consistent with the characteristics of pop-ups. We believe that, in total, these sectors likely exceed $5 billion, perhaps by a large magnitude.

So while it is still difficult to accurately portray the size of the overall pop-up market in the United States, PopUp Republic has been able to evaluate sufficient data and compilations to calculate that the size of the market is in the area

(continued)

(*continued*)

of $45 to $50 billion. As reference points, the total annual retail market in the United States is approximately $4.5 trillion, and the size of the online retail market is about $300 billion. So by comparison, the size of the pop-up market is relatively small, though certainly significant. But while offline "brick-and-mortar" retail is stagnating, resulting in corporate contractions and smaller store sizes, pop-ups are expanding and reflect a steadily growing trend of consumer preferences for local, handmade, exclusive product lines and favoring personal "shopping experiences" over homogeneous, predictable shopping options.

CITATIONS
Food Trucks

- Intuit estimates that the food truck industry will be $2.7 billion in 2017.
- The National Restaurant Association estimated sales of about $650 million in 2012.
- IBISWorld estimates that the food street vendors market, which is mostly food trucks, is currently a $1 billion market.
- From those three calculations, PopUp Republic estimates that 2014 sales will approximate $1 billion for food trucks. Based on Intuit's forecasted annual growth percentages, the starting point of $650 million in 2012, and the conclusion that 2014 will generate $1 billion, it means the pace of growth is a little faster than that projected by Intuit, so we went with $3 billion in 2017.

Farmers Markets

- U.S. Department of Agriculture has already been cited as the source.

Yard Sales

- Arizona State University study in 2010 estimated the size of the unregulated yard sale market to be $600 million to $1 billion (https://asunews.asu.edu/20100304_Things_We_Sell). Since four years have elapsed and we tend to think numbers in this area are under-reported, we go with $1 billion in 2014.

Flea Markets

- $30 billion estimate is provided by the National Flea Market Association: www.fleamarkets.org

Others

- These would include "pure" pop-up shops, restaurants, and supper clubs; food/drink/entertainment festivals; open artist studios; craft fairs; one-off classes; and other smaller segments that are consistent with the characteristics of pop-ups. We believe that, in total, these sectors likely exceed $5 billion, perhaps by a large magnitude.

The Case for Pop-Up Urbanism as a Tool to Vitalize Local Economies

Case Study: Christchurch, New Zealand

In February 2011, New Zealand's second largest city, Christchurch, was hit by a major earthquake. 185 people were killed, many buildings were destroyed, and the damage is estimated now to have cost NZ$40 billion. Economists predict that it will take between 50 and 100 years for New Zealand to completely recover.

The central commercial district was particularly hit hard by the February 22 catastrophe. City Mall, the main pedestrian mall in Christchurch, was virtually destroyed and cordoned off, with 80 percent of the district having been demolished.

On October 29, a mere eight months after disaster struck, City Mall re-opened, albeit with a very different look and identity. The new iteration of City Mall was built from shipping

(continued)

31

(*continued*)
containers. The shipping containers were retrofitted to accommodate an initial roster of 27 shops. This was not meant to be a long-term solution. Rather, the strategy was to bootstrap the mall's recovery through this temporary measure, giving birth to "Re:START," a pop-up mall whose aim was to accelerate the revitalization of commerce in central Christchurch.

Re:START was the brainchild of Christchurch's Property and Building Owners group, who recognized that the revival of downtown commerce was vital not only for its economic well-being, but also for its psychological well-being. Re-building the city with permanent, earthquake-resistant structures would take years, and leaders felt that the people needed something to happen more quickly.

Re:START was an immediate hit, and the container mall continues to receive worldwide acclaim for its accomplishment. It now houses over 50 businesses along with market booths and street entertainers. Besides spearheading the economic revival of the city, Re:START has been the central force behind the resuscitation of Christchurch's tourist industry as well, becoming a "must-see" for world travelers.

With such widespread devastation, both financially and emotionally, how much did it cost to construct the Re:START container mall and begin to put Christchurch's business scene back on sound economic footing?

Re:START was funded with an interest-free loan of NZ$3,368,523 from the Earthquake Appeal Trust, supplemented by a $300,000 contribution from New Zealand's ASB Bank.

Case Study: Camden, U.K.

The London Borough of Camden is located in northern London, abutting Central London to its south. Its local governing authority is the Camden London Borough Council, overseeing a number of directorates. But its local businesses also undertake a robust approach toward developing and promoting initiatives that would help local commerce.

In 2009, faced with myriad local economic challenges, including an unsustainably high number of storefront vacancies, Camden Town Unlimited (CTU) was appointed by the business community to implement programs to upgrade the local commercial performance. Among them was a Pop-Up Shop program whose aim was to transform empty stores into vibrant platforms for start-ups and boutiques.

In its first year, the CTU acquired three empty retail venues and filled them with a rotation of pop-up shops. During that first year, all three storefronts were able to attract long-term tenants, the community began to re-connect with the local business retail establishment, and jobs were created. Since then, dozens more vacancies have been filled with pop-ups, offering a wide variety of galleries, stores, incubator space, art, and handmade artisanal merchandise.

Pop-ups have now become a line item in the Camden town budget, providing low-cost tools through which permanent tenants are cultivated, businesses are grown, and community benefits are reaped.

Case Study: Oakland, California (U.S.A.)

Popuphood is a community-based organization that was founded to curate and activate previously vacant spaces in Oakland—block by block. It is a movement to energize local economic development through the use of pop-ups in order to create jobs, provide pathways to permanent leases, and enhance the attractiveness of urban living.

Popuphood was started in September 2011 as a grassroots attempt to bring life to an urban area that had continually been marked by high unemployment and storefront vacancies.

(continued)

(*continued*)

With the help of a small grant, Popuphood was able to offer five new retail shops—ranging from a bicycle shop to a metalsmith to a jewelry-maker—six months of free rent at previously empty storefronts, all located on one block. The spaces had been empty for over a year.

Since that time, dozens of new shops point to Popuphood as having been the catalyst to a brick-by-brick, block-by-block revival that has helped launch local businesses, create permanent retail tenants, and turn previously avoided streets and neighborhoods into popular destinations for both local and out-of-the-area visitors.

These three case studies are examples of how those charged with revitalizing local and even hyper-local communities are utilizing pop-ups to effect positive change.

When trying to understand what is propelling pop-ups forward as an emerging retail trend, one usually starts off by pointing to the "shop local," "DIY," "handmade" preferences shoppers are embracing. Or they may put the focus on the desire for exclusivity and the desire for a shopping *experience*. Or fingers might point to general currents in the economy, where entrepreneurialism on one hand and the desire to mitigate risk and large commitments on the other, have led to the growth of pop-ups as a natural solution.

But the pop-up trend must also give credit to the community of economic development professionals. There are thousands of economic development officers, on the state, regional, municipal, and even community levels, whose task it is to somehow foster economic growth in their geographic areas. And they are being asked to do this while hamstrung with tighter and tighter budgets. There is literally competition for every dollar they have to spend.

Economic development professionals also have several constituents who look to them for assistance: local merchants, local consumers, commercial property owners, and people wanting to start businesses. Sometimes their interests coincide; sometimes they conflict. Officials have to find the right balance among them all—not an easy job.

Then along came the pop-up movement. Suddenly, there was an inexpensive—sometime no cost at all—way to connect several interests all at once. Often, pop-ups are able to provide a one-size-fits-all solution to all of these distinct groups, the ultimate win-win scenario.

Some examples:

- *Venues*—When one thinks of pop-up venues, the first thought that comes to mind are vacant storefronts. Pop-up shops that move into empty spaces, even for a short period of time, help the landlord in a variety of ways. They provide incremental income—perhaps not a huge windfall, but usually enough to cover such expenses as utilities, insurance, and other fixed costs. They provide staging—it is far better for a landlord to be able to show his or her space active and alive, as being able to support local business, than empty and perhaps even a "loser." Perhaps best of all, they provide a conduit to permanent lessees, for it is not uncommon for the pop-up to become permanent, and for the pop-up merchant to become a permanent lessee!
- *Merchants*—Pop-ups help merchants in several ways. The most obvious one is that they are relatively inexpensive ways for vendors, designers, collectors, and makers to test out the market for their goods and services without having to quit their jobs, mortgage their homes, and go blindly into a new enterprise. Pop-ups are great testing grounds for new businesses and start-ups. And they are exclusive outlets for artisans to actually showcase and commercialize their talents.

Pop-ups also help already-established businesses from a couple of perspectives. First, an exciting pop-up, one that is drawing new foot traffic from consumers who visit with an intention to spend money, often spill over into nearby establishments as well. A buzz is created, and pop-up shoppers often stop at nearby eateries for a snack or lunch or to expand their shopping expeditions to include other stores near the pop-up shop.

And in a newly discovered benefit, many stores and boutiques are using pop-ups as their own marketing resource, making space within the confines of their stores for third-party pop-ups (and charging them rent!) and themselves gaining from the pedestrian traffic that is drawn to check out the new pop-up in the area.

- *Consumers*—Consumers have shown that they love pop-ups, in all of their forms. Whether seasonal farmers and flea markets; food trucks and food truck festivals; pop-up parklets and flash mobs; yard sales; one-off entertainment and classes; or "conventional" pop-up dinners and pop-up stores, pop-ups lend an air of excitement to otherwise static shopping, dining, and entertainment options. And this benefits everyone, including the communities that host the pop-up events.

As Baby Boomers retire from their full-time occupations, and as Millennials enter an ever-tightening job market, economic development professionals are put under greater pressure to find local business opportunities for their constituent populations. At the same time, these same officials are asked to do their jobs under tighter budgetary constraints. Pop-up initiatives have become a low-cost resource that cities, large and small, are turning to with greater frequency as a means to promote local merchants, customers, and neighborhoods.

Interview with Florence Hardy, an Urban Economic Development Professional about Pop-Ups

FLORENCE HARDY IS the manager of the Small Business Development Center of the Chicagoland Chamber of Commerce. Ms. Hardy is well-versed in the challenges that professionals and communities are facing in seeking to bootstrap their neighborhoods into economic health.

Q: What is your background?

A graduate of the John Marshall Law School, I have been a successful business consultant for more than eight years. I have a master's degree in business administration with a focus on entrepreneurship from DePaul University and received a bachelor's degree in business administration from Howard University. I worked for the City of Chicago, DePaul University, and had my own law practice before joining the Chicagoland Chamber of Commerce as

(continued)

37

(*continued*)
manager of the Small Business Development Center. I have lived and studied in Chicago, Illinois, Washington, D.C., and Berlin, Germany, and currently reside in Flossmoor, Illinois, with my husband, Michael.

Q: Can you provide examples (either in Chicago or elsewhere) of how pop-ups have made a difference in communities?

While not seen as an area in need, the rents in the loop have resulted in a number of vacancies on prime streets. The Pop Up Art Loop program sponsored by the Chicago Loop Alliance was the first program to address this issue. In addition to providing access to art that would otherwise have been hidden without access, these art spaces bring life to areas of the loop that are deserted at night.

Q: What are some of the challenges associated with starting pop-ups?

The negotiations with landlords can be difficult at times. Specifically, as it relates to the rebate they receive for having vacancies. Getting them to see the value of hosting a pop-up space in an otherwise empty venue is not as cut and dry as it sounds like it would be.

Q: Do you see local governments establishing protocols/ licenses needed to operate pop-ups? As they become more "accepted" in economies, this is one of the biggest questions that we are asked.

I hope that, as pop-ups get more popular, an easy licensing or exemption from license process will be determined. Having worked for the City for a number of years, any legislation that addresses this issue will be long and likely not occur until 2017, if at all.

Q: How have pop-ups influenced your work?

Pop-ups are the MVP [minimally viable product] for retail operations, and I encourage all of my retail clients to try pop-ups first before making the leap into full-time retail operations. Specifically, hosting pop-ups is a primary part of the retail education program we are planning here at the Chamber and we will require each student to operate at least two pop-up stores during the program.

Q: Why do economic development officials (and other government officials) like pop-ups?

Pop-ups are a quick way to check the economic viability of a location without much capital investment. While it takes time to market and advertise the pop-up, the same would be true for a long-term tenant. By using pop-ups, officials can verify whether certain concepts will work in a given area and continue to alter until the right concept is found.

Q: Is there a difference in perception between landlords (property owners/managers) and merchants? Specifically, pop-ups provide different benefits for each side; does one side typically put up more resistance than the other?

Absolutely, there is a difference. Landlords generally are a lot more resistant to the idea of pop-ups, as their goal is to attract a long-term tenant, not multiple short-term tenants, as multiple tenants require more work. However, the value proposition for landlords is that by allowing pop-ups, they are allowing potential long-term tenants to "try before they buy," which could mean happier, longer-term tenants in the end. This value just has to be explained to landlords over and over again.

Q: What type of regulation is there for non-traditional space (pop-up shops/restaurants within existing businesses; stores-within-stores/restaurants-within-restaurants; personal residences, etc.)?

Right now, there is very little regulation regarding the shops/restaurants within existing shops/restaurants and it isn't a bad idea to keep it that way. However, using a personal residence for business

(continued)

(*continued*)
purposes is regulated heavily (at least in the City of Chicago) and most, if not all, anticipated uses fall outside of what is permitted.

Q: How do you see the industry growing over the next year? What new challenges will present themselves?

I think the industry will grow gangbusters, and more businesses are looking to try out concepts with consumers before investing tons of money into a brick and mortar. With that, I think regulation will come, and that will be the major challenge that the industry will have to face.

Q: What is the greatest pop-up you've ever heard about?

That is a good question. While one individual pop-up does not come to mind, I think pop-up events are best. For example, there is a company called Pop-Up Wed that performs elopement ceremonies in awesome locations. Those are the kinds of situations that make for memorable experiences, whether one is a participant or a spectator.

Becoming a "Popupreneur"

LIKE EVERY NEW venture, a careful and organized plan is required in order to execute a successful pop-up. I am a firm believer that people can make money from almost any serious endeavor—they just need a winning mindset, a passion for their product or service, and a "never fail" attitude.

It is easy to steer off the tracks and get caught up in failures, or to be distracted from achieving your goals. This section will help you stay on the right path and develop the tools that you will need to organize and achieve success as a "popupreneur."

Are You a Good Candidate to Host a Pop-Up?

Back in the latter decades of the 1900s, one of America's leading serial entrepreneurs was a Massachusetts businessman named George Naddaff. He is most widely known as a successful multiple franchise owner of Kentucky Fried Chicken, for the expansion of the fledgling Boston Chicken into a national chain, and for the founding of Living & Learning Centers, which he sold to KinderCare.

But it was a lesser-known enterprise, VR Business Brokers, that perhaps suited him the most. Naddaff was a deal-maker and a grower of businesses, and VR fit his personality to a T. Built up in the 1970s and early 1980s, his concept was to take the mom-and-pop industry, known as business brokerage, where a middleman would help sellers market and sell their businesses to prospective buyers and create a unified national network.

Naddaff's role in the company, besides founding chairman and CEO, was to recruit franchisees who would open VR business brokerage offices across the company—something he was very good at (he ultimately sold his 300-office/3,000-broker network to a British investment house). Every Friday morning, a group of potential franchisees would assemble in a large conference room at

VR headquarters. Once seated, there would suddenly appear from a side entrance toward the front of the room a dapper 50-something-year-old man, who wouldn't just walk in . . . he would run in, brimming with enthusiasm, and advance to the podium.

As Naddaff addressed the crowd, he stressed one main point: that next to owning a home, the pinnacle of "The American Dream" had always been, and still was, owning one's own business. That was the essence of his message and sales pitch: the target market for a VR business franchise was virtually *anybody*, as owning and running a business was what people truly wanted in life.

Flash forward 30 plus years to today. We live in a different era, not just chronologically but socially as well. Women and minorities have made great strides in climbing the corporate ladder, the technological age is upon us, and the two largest demographic groups are Millennials and Baby Boomers.

While it may no longer be the case that almost *everyone* wants to own and operate a business, is that still a sentiment shared by a large segment of the public? The answer is . . . yes!

According to a recent survey conducted by the University of Phoenix, if you're under 30 years old, you probably do want to run your own business. Out of the 1,600 adults surveyed, 63 percent of people in their twenties either owned their own businesses or wanted to someday, and of those who were not already entrepreneurs, 55 percent hoped to be in the future.

That's a compelling number, but it is even more significant when you realize that 30 years ago, starting and owning a business was totally out of the question for most of those American dreamers. It would have involved quitting a job, taking a second mortgage on the house, risking it all without testing the market, and making a full-time commitment to the new endeavor. Very few had that as even a remote possibility to consider.

But now there is another option, a way to launch a business without quitting a job, without needing a lot of capital, being able to test the market, and only submitting to a temporary, manageable commitment of time and money: pop-ups! Although the name "pop-up" might sound too whimsical to be taken seriously, it is, in fact, a movement that is far more sensible as a launch pad for businesses than in the golden age of VR Business Brokerage some 30 plus years ago, when such an option didn't exist.

And how about the Baby Boomers, of which there are currently 76 *million*? According to that same University of Phoenix survey, 26 percent of those over 60 not already running their own businesses had a desire to do so, even during their retirement years! That's over 20 million Boomers!

This generation, whether young or old, is witnessing the lure of the start-up culture that surrounds us all. Couple that with the advent of pop-ups in the form of pop-up shops, restaurants, farmers markets, food trucks, flea markets, and others, and the opportunities to follow your dreams become readily approachable—and hard to resist.

And not only are pop-ups meant for artisanal handiworks. They are also meant for collections, and perhaps most of all, for ideas, skills, education, and entertainment. Story slams, poetry readings, yoga and fitness classes, mixology lessons, palm reading, music . . . there is no end to what the subject matter could be. We heard of a couple, both teachers, who moved to Florida to take on new teaching jobs, only to discover once there that the jobs had evaporated. Needing an income until new teaching jobs could be secured, they turned to a particular expertise they had developed— making jellies and preserves. They bottled them, opened up a once-a-week roadside stand, and gained such an avid following that this pop-up sustained them until they were able to gain the teaching jobs they wanted.

Whether you are a candidate to host a successful pop-up doesn't depend on whether you have the time, or the money, or the talent. You have all of that. It depends solely on whether you go ahead and do it.

A Day in the Life of a Popupreneur

ONE BEAUTIFUL THING about running your own business is that you are your own boss. You dictate when you do and do not work, how much money you make, and the type of products or services that you offer. On the other hand, you and you alone are responsible for the success or failure of your pop-up, and that can be scary at times.

No matter what type of product you are selling or service you are offering, you need to know it cold. If you do not have knowledge or passion about your product(s), customers can tell immediately. After all, the people who directly determine whether or not you monetize from your pop-up are your customers.

Choosing a Concept

You CANNOT HAVE a pop-up without a concept. Sometimes, this is easy. If you're a jewelry designer, it makes sense that you open a shop that showcases your designs. Similarly, if you're a chef, perhaps you have training in one particular type of cuisine, and your pop-up restaurant is your chance to show your chops (or whatever cuisine you specialize in). Others, however, might have a different set of skills and trying to decide which one makes a good business can be tricky.

The right concept is certainly dependent on your expertise or interests, but there are also other factors to consider:

- *Time of Year:* Pop-ups that open in the winter could, perhaps, have a holiday theme
- *Neighborhood:* If you find a space in an "artsy" part of town, maybe it makes sense to create a pop-up art gallery featuring the works of local artists, makers, and crafters.
- *Type of Space:* You need a space that ultimately suits your needs. If you're creating a pop-up restaurant, common sense dictates that you should not open it in a venue that is built for retail. Similarly, if you are a fashion designer, you need somewhere that can hold mannequins, has clothing racks, enough shelving for you to display your goods, and perhaps a fitting room.

Creating a Concept vs. Creating a Concept That Sells

THE WORST POSSIBLE situation for any business owner is if you build it and no one comes. As I mentioned earlier, everyone has some unique skill, hobby, or interest, but how do you know whether that can translate into an idea that can make you money? There is an old *Friends* episode where character Joey Tribbiani finds his "identical hand twin" and concocts a plan to quit his job and hit the road as a hand model. That is an example of what not to do. If you are a maker—someone who prints jewelry from a 3D printer, or a photographer, or a designer or ceramic artist—customers would generally have interest in what you're creating. If you are a baker and want to teach a class, as long as it's something that would interest the public, then you have a good shot at making money from it.

Pop-ups provide an incredible opportunity for individuals to create alternative sources of income at a reasonable cost. Opportunities are limitless when it comes to what customers respond to and what can generate significant revenues.

Being able to identify what types of products customers respond to is the key to any successful business, and tailoring your pop-up to meet demand is also critical. As long as you have a plan and can execute it, you will have pop-up success.

For those who know that they want to try their hand at launching a pop-up, but are struggling to find an idea of what to sell or what type of service to provide, we'll make it a little easier for you by putting forth some possibilities. Perhaps they will strike a nerve, or maybe they will spark a totally different idea, one that is right up your alley:

Design

- 3D printing
- Fashion
- Jewelry
- Visual

Arts and Crafts

- Animation
- Calligraphy
- Caricature
- Ceramics and pottery
- Drawing
- Graffiti
- Illumination
- Illustration
- Mosaic
- Quilting
- Performance
- Photography
- Sculptures
- Tapestry

Collections and Galleries

- Maps
- Stamps
- Art

- Postcards
- Baseball cards
- Pokémon
- Legos

General Skills

- Puppetry
- Clowns
- Singing
- Poetry
- Dancing
- Music
- Writing
- Magic

Dining

- Pop-up restaurants
- Pop-up cafes
- Exclusive dining experiences
- Supper clubs
- Food trucks
- Food and drink festivals

Types of Pop-Up Restaurants

- American
- Appetizers
- Asian/Latin Fusion
- Bagels
- Baked goods
- Barbecue
- Brazilian
- Breakfast
- Cajun
- Caribbean
- Chinese

- Chocolate
- Christmas
- Crepes
- Cuban
- Desserts
- Drinks
- Dumplings
- Easter
- Entrees
- Filipino
- French
- Fusion
- Gluten-free
- Greek
- Gyros
- Hawaiian
- Health
- Indian
- Italian
- Jamaican
- Japanese
- Kids
- Korean
- Kosher
- Latin
- Meat
- Mediterranean
- Mexican
- Organic
- Pakistani
- Passover
- Peruvian
- Peruvian
- Pies

- Polish
- Poultry
- Romanian
- Sandwiches
- Seafood
- Soup
- Southern
- Spanish
- Sushi
- Swedish
- Tapas
- Thai
- Thanksgiving
- Turkish
- Venezuelan
- Wings

While not a complete list by any means, I hope it will create some inspiration and help you decide the type of pop-up that would best meet your skills, interests, and the needs of your potential customers.

Once you have your concept, everything else should easily fall into place, as long as you put in the time to prepare. Realize that the amount of time, and the elements involved in launching and hosting a pop-up, are not nearly as comprehensive and time-consuming as a permanent business involves. That is another benefit of starting with a pop-up. But that doesn't mean you can totally avoid the planning process. It is necessary, and it can make a huge difference.

As I mention later in this book, it is a good idea to create events surrounding your pop-up to drive foot traffic. It is easier to create events once you know what products or services will be provided at your pop-up, and you will also be able to determine the types of licenses, insurance, and signage you will need as you begin to set it up.

What to Expect

THE NORMAL DAY for a pop-up organizer varies based on the category (shop, restaurant, supper club, event) and the location (stand-alone space, store-within-a-store, restaurant-within-a-restaurant, etc.). Like any retail business, its day-to-day operation is a full-time commitment, if only for that day.

Not only are you the one making the product or providing the service, but unless you have a staff (which can be costly), you are also the CMO, CFO, COO, CTO, director of business development, and head intern, all in one. Be prepared for this. It is important that, before you go into the planning and development process of your pop-up, you know what you are getting into.

How to Manage It All

FOCUS ON YOUR strengths first. If you're a numbers person, concentrate on the accounting. This is important anyway, since it is crucial that you have a grasp of your projected revenues and expenses, but if it's something you're good at, set up a spreadsheet so that you can be in charge of tracking this throughout the duration of your pop-up.

For those areas that are not your strength or for which you don't think you'll have enough time to handle, look for outside help. There are companies that can provide services on your behalf at reasonable costs. One such area that is often overlooked is marketing. Because pop-ups are short-term, operators feel they can dispense with marketing as a priority. Just hang up the sign and open for business. In fact, especially when it comes to pop-ups, the opposite is true. Pop-ups have none of the marketing weapons that are usually available for retail and dining establishments—no advertising, no prior foot traffic, no attractive buildouts or signage, no prior word of mouth, no coupons—almost none of the resources. This means that extra attention has to be paid to marketing your pop-up, using whatever means are available.

What you'll be hearing and reading about most often when it comes to marketing and promoting pop-ups is social media marketing. This is an accurate assessment. There is no better way for an upcoming or ongoing pop-up to connect with the public and to spread the word than through strategic, consistent social media marketing campaigns. If, along with all of the other tasks at hand, you are able to use social media marketing effectively by yourself and you have the network necessary to spread the word, then that is a great situation. But most pop-up hosts don't have that luxury. This is a great area to outsource. At the risk of sounding too self-serving, this is an area of expertise at which my company, PopUp Republic, can offer you tremendous help. We have tailor-made our pop-up marketing services for the pop-up community and offer marketing and promotional services to pop-ups that are looking for that sort of help. We take that burden off of you and act as your marketing department to drive business to your pop-up.

Many companies offer a variety of complementary services for your pop-up, designed to reduce the load off of your shoulders—temporary staffing agencies, bookkeepers, furniture and fixture rental companies, sign makers, carpenters, and others. We live in a world that offers and requires specialization—if you can't do it well, someone can.

One more note that bears repeating: Don't get discouraged. I know that it's easier said than done, but the pop-up process can really be a lot of fun, especially if you are able to compartmentalize those areas that aren't fun. All of the side stuff—payroll, securing licenses, establishing bank accounts, shopping for furniture and fixtures, finding a space, etc.—comes with the territory. If you have the budget to hire a staff, that will certainly help with delegation and allocation, but even if you don't, you need to look at a pop-up as a "mini-business" and expect to run it as such. Perhaps there won't be peaks and valleys, but there are likely to be occasional hills and gullies.

The Day-to-Day

ONCE YOU ARE open, here are a few simple things that may be expected of you when you first arrive:

- Unlock the doors and keep them propped open to create a more welcoming atmosphere (subject to weather, of course) for your customers.
- Depending on the type of pop-up, turn on music and have it play in the background (not too loud!) throughout the day.
- Make sure there is cash in the cash box or register.
- Keep track of employee hours and hold them accountable.
- Clean your space, making sure it's a welcoming environment for customers.
- Clean bathrooms, kitchens, and/or common areas.
- Make sure your products are arranged in an aesthetically pleasing way.

As you gain more experience, you will develop policies and procedures that will become second-nature for you and part of your daily routine. Ultimately, it is important that you create an environment that is conducive to handling multiple customers at one time—if you're a chef, this is a bit different, as usually pop-up dining concepts are seated and ticketed meals, but for retailers, if you are selling products that are scattered about your shop and require explanation, it might be wise to hire hourly staff (or have friends or family help out) so that multiple people with knowledge of your brand and offerings can provide an experience for customers and make the sale.

We hear from pop-up organizers all the time that, although they have achieved some level of success, there is far more management and overseeing involved than simply providing an exceptional customer service experience for your clients or directly handling your products. Depending on the scale and scope of your pop-up, you will also need to manage your staff, create and organize grand opening events (and other supplemental events) in order to make your pop-up a destination and spectacle, and act as your own bookkeeper and handle finances and expense reports.

Therefore, it is advised that you have at least one other person to work with you who can serve as a jack of all trades and interact with customers, field questions from staff, or educate the public about your products.

What Is Success?

ARGUABLY, THE MOST important thing that you can do when you are first thinking about your pop-up is to determine your end game. What is your goal? For some, it is to generate significant revenues. For chefs, perhaps it is to experiment with new menus and test new locations. For designers, maybe they want to see how responsive customers are to their work, before potentially opening up their own galleries or boutiques.

As a society, we often become bogged down by cultural pressures to make as much money as possible. For first-time pop-up organizers, this is the best advice that I can give: Don't worry about the money. Success is all about expectations. More than likely, your first pop-up may provide you with meaningful income—or it may not. You will see that there are things you would do differently a second time (and you should definitely plan on hosting another pop-up—you'll be amazed how much easier, and probably more lucrative, it is the second time around). If you go into your first one with the *expectation* that you are doing it for a reason other than the money, namely, that you might make some money but you will be obtaining an incredible learning experience for the next pop-up you host, you have a higher likelihood of completing the process from start to finish and achieving both customer and personal satisfaction at the end of the process.

No matter what type of pop-up you open, you need experience in order to have the confidence that you are going down the right track. If you are opening a pop-up restaurant, you may not need to have previously been a professional chef, but you should have some knowledge of food costs, area demographics (familiarizing yourself with median incomes in your area will allow you to gauge how much customers will spend), and setting a menu. If you are opening a clothing pop-up, previous retail experience will help you interact with customers and know what to anticipate.

If one of your goals is to turn your temporary pop-up into a full-time permanent business, keep a close eye on scalability. Does your business model lend itself to expansion and growth? Do you want to just operate in one location or in multiple locations? Do you have hopes of going national, or even global? Feel free to have ambition, but start the planning process at the pop-up level, testing out procedures and protocols that can make sense at a larger scale. Create a concept that not only works as a pop-up, but also one that you can replicate on a national (or international) level. For instance, we had one client who was an accomplished chef who decided she wanted to leave her corporate gig and open a Filipino pop-up restaurant. Except, instead of operating in a single location, she created a pop-up experience in all 50 states over the course of a year. That's 50 "restaurants"; 50 opportunities to create new, loyal customers; 50 chances to make a lot of money. At the end of this journey, she had many opportunities to build on her initial pop-up model, and we are certain this will lead to a successful business for her for many years to come.

Now, I'm not suggesting you need to become that ambitious, but as you create your concept, think about those two important questions: What is my endgame? How can I make this scalable?

Customers

THE SINGLE BIGGEST indicator of how a pop-up is doing is the number of customers who attend. If it's a 30- to 90-day pop-up (or longer), it is more difficult to entice customers to come than if your pop-up takes place over a weekend or even on a single day. With proper promotion, a short-term pop-up can generate significant foot traffic and attract customers without the need for any other enticements or incentives. A longer term pop-up requires more careful planning and, depending on the type, could provide a great opportunity to incorporate your pop-up with other brands or businesses in the community.

Once your pop-up is open, no matter its duration, there are several characteristics that will make a difference:

- *Smile:* Everyone is attracted to a smile. No matter what is going on in your personal life, you have to leave all that behind and make sure it appears as though you are having the greatest day ever.
- *Customer service:* Think about the worst customer service experience you have had. We've all had them. Vow to do the opposite of that on a daily basis.
- *Confidence:* It can lure customers. If you show that you know more about your product(s) than anyone, can provide

interesting anecdotes about them, or describe, in detail, how they're made, that's interesting and something that will create a refined experience.

- **Passion:** It is so easy to tell whether or not someone cares about his or her products. Facial expressions, body language, even personality, are all indicators of passion. Show your customers that you care and they will gravitate toward your pop-up.

As a business owner, having customers spread the word on your behalf and encouraging friends to patronize your business is one of the most difficult goals to achieve, but for a pop-up, it is imperative. That's where an incredible experience matters. Good salespeople can sell ice to an Eskimo. Why? The salesperson understands the Eskimo. He or she is intuitive and treats the Eskimo like he's the most important Eskimo in the world. Even if sales aren't your strong suit, you can create an incredible, once-in-a-lifetime event by the ambiance of your pop-up. Make it a place that people think about when they leave. Do that, and you will create loyal customers who would be happy to tell others about the exclusive, exciting shopping or dining experience they just had.

Another way to expand your reach if you are opening a physical retail pop-up is to create a simultaneous online presence. Your offline pop-up will attract a local clientele. Your online pop-up could attract a national clientele. If you're a pop-up shop owner, we strongly encourage you to create a corresponding online store, probably on PopUps Across America (which is operated exclusively for pop-up shops by PopUp Republic) or on e-commerce sites such as Shopify and Etsy. This will allow your products to be available for a longer period of time, beyond the typical hyperlocal reach. Offering discounts or promo codes is a great way to gain followers on social media while also creating customers who can make purchases in your store. Running contests and giveaways enhances your connection with customers and makes your online brand just as attractive as your physical pop-up.

The Execution

ONCE YOU CREATE your plan, you are ready to begin implementing it. How effectively you execute can ultimately determine the success or failure of your pop-up. Because of their temporary nature, it's important that whatever type of pop-up you're organizing, you adequately promote it ahead of time to build buzz and create interest. This section will dive into the three segments of pop-ups—shops, restaurants, and spaces—and help make your concept a reality.

Pop-Up Shops

DESPITE BEING A relatively new concept in the United States, pop-ups have actually evolved pretty drastically over the last few years. When the term "pop-up" first began being culturally accepted as a temporary retail or dining establishment, they often opened in vacant storefronts located primarily in major cities around the country. As soon as local economies started to struggle, economic development officials began searching for creative ways to utilize all types of space—people needed jobs, vacancies were at an all-time high, and with the development of online websites like Etsy, Pinterest, and eBay, "makers" and "collectors" were beginning to appear everywhere.

It makes sense that this led to the emergence of pop-ups in North America. As small designers began to open pop-ups in cities and towns throughout the country, large brands took notice. The first "big box" store that truly embraced the concept was Target. Because of its international presence, it didn't need to use pop-ups as a means to test new markets; rather, it saw that consumers were responding to small, locally handmade products and brands, and it began renting out portions of its stores across the country to independent designers who created complementary offerings. Dubbed "The Shops at Target," this series appeared in more than 100 stores throughout North America during the holidays of 2013. This was the first occurrence of what has been a drastic pivot by large chain stores. Gone are the days when people visit department stores and load up on all of their needed day-to-day wares.

E-commerce has made a major dent in the business of big box stores, and they are often trying to create new incentives for customers to get out of the house and visit their brick-and-mortar locations. The Shops at Target was Target's realization that the more they embraced the pop-up concept by welcoming smaller brands into their stores (and the P.R. buzz it generated), the more customers would visit. This model is the opposite of the traditional pop-up—people often just assume that they are for small brands to experiment with a physical presence, which is true; however, they are clearly a mechanism that can be implemented by big box stores on a national level to drive incremental foot traffic and enhance customer loyalty.

Online "e-tailers," such as Amazon, Nike, Zappos, and Microsoft, are also realizing that customers crave a "touch and feel" experience, and they have begun creating experiential pop-up concepts in major cities throughout the country. Some online brands have determined that having a national physical retail presence to go hand-in-hand with their national online presence can create an enhanced "discovery" process for their customers—and they're utilizing pop-ups to do this.

Pop-ups provide an inexpensive alternative to retailers of all types who do not have the large marketing budgets, big buildout capability, or existing foot traffic typically associated with permanent locations. Also, given their temporary nature, a lot of the risk is mitigated because of their "here today, gone tomorrow" type of atmosphere. This is also a big draw for customers. In 2014, we saw customers embrace "FOMO"—the fear of missing out—and pop-ups are a classic example of an event that provides a sense of urgency and call to action for consumers.

Virtually any type of space can be used for a pop-up shop. For instance, we have seen pop-up shops within permanent stores (similar to the Target concept described previously; essentially, these are "stores within stores"). This can be as simple as merchants renting out a portion of their permanent stores to pop-up shop organizers, or even renting some shelf space, window space, or their entire store to the organizer during hours when their stores are otherwise closed (allowing the permanent store proprietors to make money from their shops even during off-hours). For the pop-up organizers, this model allows them to open their pop-up without many fixed expenses besides rent (and perhaps insurance, a requirement that is up to the lessor). It also gives them existing foot traffic to capitalize on, as the permanent store likely has its own set of customers who visit on a consistent basis, and thus will also visit the pop-up.

Pop-ups are especially helpful for the individual artisan who is trying to build a brand. The short-term nature and relatively low costs associated with hosting a pop-up, and the natural curiosity that a pop-up elicits, helps the individual artisans offset a low marketing budget and a lack of public awareness for their products.

We have also seen a large increase in governments that subsidize the use of pop-ups as a means to revitalize certain areas of their cities and communities. For example, Popuphood is one of the first "government subsidized pop-up projects" in the United States, filling six vacant storefronts in Old Oakland (California) with eight different retailers, resulting in increased foot traffic, enhanced safety, and a vibrant local economy (and a few of the retailers even signed long-term leases once their pop-ups ended!). This concept created a buzz around a specific area that had been dormant for some time. Customers are interested in finding out what's happening, brands are interested in participating because of the customer base it can lead to, and it may even capture the attention of the local media, who likely would be interested in anything that revitalizes communities, creates jobs, and boosts economies.

Fly Guy Brand Is an Apparel Company Based in Colorado, Started by Teenage Brothers Austin and Preston Anguilm. Their Pop-Up Shop Opened in 2014.

Interview with Greg Spielberg, Founder of Imagination in Space

GREG SPIELBERG IS a seasoned "pop-up veteran" who has created several concepts as a means to revitalize communities and promote the works of makers, designers, and artisans. Through his New York City–based initiative, Imagination in Space, he has worked with some of the most iconic brands to create incredible pop-up experiences.

> **Q: Discuss the concept of Imagination in Space. How did it get started?**
>
> *I launched Imagination in Space in April 2013 after cutting my teeth for two years with Openhouse Gallery in Manhattan. At Openhouse, we pioneered the pop-up movement by saying, "You know what? We have 4,500 square feet of space with all the things you'd need in a retail space—WiFi, Sonos speakers, cleaning, insurance, staff, big windows for decals, A/V—but we're a blank canvas." Year-over-year revenue was tremendous, and we had clients*
>
> (continued)

(*continued*)

from Audi creating an architectural exhibit during New Museum's Ideas City festival, to Heineken creating a summer series targeting Latino creatives, to Jay Z and Kanye West launching "Watch the Throne" there, rather than at Best Buy. Over two years, I created hundreds of pop-ups; we built a big community and generated press more than 500 times. My favorite projects there were an indoor pop-up park and the world's first 3D printing shop. We built experiences and sold products inside here and there, but at the end of the day, we created creative nonfiction stories that were open to all.

After two years, I felt I wanted to bring the story-driven pop-up model to everyone, anywhere, not just at one space. We kicked off leading the international media campaign for Yazmany Arboleda's "10,000 Balloons for Kabul," where the public artist gave pink balloons to citizens of the war-torn country. The one-day pop-up produced press on six continents. In fall 2013, we were sponsored by a not-for-profit arts group to create an art show in London. "American Dreams," a New York City Pop-Up in London, featured NYC artists and provided quick, friendly art sales for busy media and health professionals in the Fitzrovia neighborhood. We attracted enough attention to the empty space that Pret a Manger moved in soon thereafter. In May 2014, we created "The Allies," a new modern art gallery featuring artists from the U.K. and U.S. sponsored by We Are Pop-Up and Martenero (a watch company). The Allies rethought the art gallery for the post-Instagram age. We hosted innovation dinners in the evening and yoga in the morning. Out of an empty space, we generated $25,000 in sales.

Last fall and through January 2015, we worked with New York City Economic Development Corporation on the five-borough "Next Top Makers" tour. The goal was to map out, showcase, and promote next-gen manufacturers in all five boroughs. We were the first company to create a five-borough tour and generated 60 press mentions, a few thousand social media impressions, and a new contract with NYCEDC. In March, we created the first bone broth festival in collaboration with Howard Hughes Corp at South Street Seaport.

Q: What is your background?

Journalist who fell in love with innovation—shifts in mindset that create more collaborative, sustainable economies. I wrote for BusinessWeek, Bloomberg, Harvard's Nieman Lab, and others, always exploring new, better ways of doing business. I pitched my editor at Bloomberg about Open House and joined their team because I wanted to help businesses and understand the language and values of real estate owners in NYC. There's nothing more valuable in top cities than square footage.

Q: There are definitely some economic advantages to pop-ups. How do they benefit organizers, especially in large metropolitan areas like New York City, Los Angeles, or San Francisco?

People value people and real experiences most. Telling an interesting story or trying to create buzz purely online is inefficient. When it is efficient and based on an algorithm like, say, BuzzFeed and Gawker, you often end up with native advertising that doesn't benefit business much. Why not create an innovation pop-up like the Wired Store, or a festival like New York Mag's Vulture Festival instead of sponsoring a silly post? Big-city pop-up organizers can take advantage of the local network effect and drive foot traffic through events, word of mouth, and social media.

Q: What is the "perfect" space for a pop-up organizer?

Ground floor, 600 to 1,500 square feet, big glass windows, well-painted, WiFi, nice fixtures, good sound system, easy mobile POS, and a desk for staff.

Q: How do pop-up organizers look for inspiration when they plan and operate their pop-ups? If I am a quilt maker, the product(s) I am making or the process by which I make them might not be too exciting, so how do I make my pop-up shop enticing, interesting and a "fear-of-missing-out" experience?

(continued)

(continued)

Create something visually beautiful. Create knowledge-based events like panels, discussions, brainstorms. Teach people how to quilt and propel existing quilt makers to do something even more special.

Q: What are some goals that you have for the growth of the industry? For me, I would love to see more government regulation and involvement, perhaps by creating a set of rules, licenses, and permits exclusively for pop-ups.

Ease the liquor permitting rules. A lot of people get caught up in that. Also, absolutely 100 percent earmark $250,000 a year to rent a few spaces in high-traffic areas for permanent pop-ups. A $5,000 a month space in a high-traffic area is crucial for developing small or online-only businesses into a full-fledged shop.

Q: What methods do you use to educate people about the various types of space that they can use for pop-ups?

Conversations, lots and lots of conversations.

Q: When you have created and executed the various pop-up concepts that Imagination in Space organizes, what has the reaction been by local governments, merchants, and community leaders? Do they all understand the concept, and do they embrace it?

People don't all understand it at the beginning, but when they go on the journey, they're hooked for life. When you create a pop-up, you're creating a seemingly fictional story where all the characters are locals.

Q: Any plans to expand the Imagination in Space concept nationally?

We worked with New Balance in Shanghai but haven't gone national yet. We'd love to work with more small towns to create retail labs to test out shared-economic shops.

Q: How does an organizer make the pop-up concept scalable?

Own the space or have a long-term lease or build a big enough following online that you can pop up anywhere and people will follow you.

Customers Interact at the "Next Top Makers" Pop-Up Shop in New York City, Sponsored by Imagination in Space.

Planning Your Pop-Up Business

Seasonality

Even though pop-ups are relatively easy to open, for some, timing is of the essence. Seasonality influences the concept, location, and duration of many pop-ups. When we first launched in 2012, we did so before pop-ups were a "thing" in the United States. Whenever we described what we did, people often were able to relate it to Halloween shops. All over the world, there is something called the "Christmas Creep," a time when retailers can begin offering their sales and other creative promotions as a means to lure customers into beginning their holiday shopping. This is also a crucial time for pop-ups, whose seasonality mirrors that of traditional retail.

The "Christmas Creep" can be a blessing for those who are experienced or truly prepared to take an influx of customers head on; it could also be a curse for those who are ill-prepared. I would advise that popupreneurs seek outside guidance from retail experts before opening pop-up shops for the holidays; while it can be perhaps more lucrative than any other time of the year, if you do not have experience with transacting and interacting with customers, it can quickly become overwhelming.

The winter months are also a time when we see an increase in artisan festivals, bazaars, and indoor farmers markets. As people travel, they love to bring back local knicknacks from wherever they are, and consumers love the "shop local" experience. Participating in an artisan fair is a great way to meet others in the industry and also sell some product to an interested customer base! A great low-cost, high-exposure opportunity.

Seasonality also relates to the weather. Keep in mind that farmers markets might be open for business from June through October, but that many of the items that customers turn to farmers markets for are not available until harvest season, so attendance might be lower in the early parts of the seasonal farmers market than later on, when more agricultural products might be available.

Insurance, Permits, and Licenses

In order to open a pop-up shop, make sure that you have the necessary paperwork filled out and submitted to the appropriate parties. Often, landlords will require general liability insurance as a condition of lease. This can be obtained through any reputable insurance broker. However, we have found that securing insurance can be more time-consuming than you would think. It never happens that a simple "binder" can automatically be put in place and that a policy can take effect within a matter of days. Start the process early. Currently, there are no "standard practices" associated with pop-up shop insurance since the industry is still emerging. Some insurance companies might resist providing coverage for your pop-up shop because of the risk involved and given the temporary nature of pop-ups; more often than not, though, a broker can find an insurer who is willing to provide coverage on a short-term basis. Explaining your business to an insurance agent is often all you'll need to do in order to obtain some sort of insurance for your pop-up.

Each city and town has its own requirements when it comes to permits and licenses associated with opening a brick-and-mortar business. You will find there is a department, and a regulation, that governs many parts of the pop-up business you want to open. Start off with the economic development and planning department. Set up a face-to-face meeting with one of their representatives and solicit their assistance in determining what licenses and permits might be required, how to navigate the system, how long the process will take, and which departments are involved. It is not a cumbersome procedure at all, but it helps to start with someone whose job entails having the answers to these questions.

Another option for those who either cannot afford their own vacant storefront or who do not want to deal with the hassles of securing all of the permits associated with opening a pop-up is the store-within-a-store concept. For example, occasionally permanent stores will sublet portions of their stores to other brands that are looking to "pop up" with similar product offerings. In this case, it is possible, based on the arranged setup between the two parties, to avoid at least some of the permitting/licensing requirements that otherwise might be mandated.

Promotion

Promoting pop-up shops can be a challenge. If you are utilizing the store-within-store concept, it actually becomes easier because you can tap into the existing clients for the store in which you are open, and it also provides you with a physical location that people are familiar with. If you are going the independent route and taking over a spot that had been vacant for a good period of time prior, it's a bit more challenging, but there are some things that you can do to help create some buzz.

For those who are planning longer-term pop-ups (30 to 90 days or more), we would advise that you create a "Grand Opening Celebration," not only to ring in your new business and retail experience, but also to generate foot traffic and allow customers to associate your shop with a particular location. Throughout the duration of the pop-up, special sales and events become centerpieces for promotional activity and are important to include.

In 2013, PopUp Republic created a holiday marketplace in Brookline, Massachusetts, where we took over several storefronts and filled them with 36 artists from the Greater Boston area (a case study appears later in the book). This was our first time actually executing a pop-up, but we gained first-hand experience as to the common pitfalls usually associated with operating a temporary retail store. One of them is the type of location in which you open. The building in which we operated had been empty for the better part of a decade, and the community just assumed it would stay empty. The biggest hurdle we faced was that, suddenly, something was there. So we created a grand opening celebration and invited local musicians and media members (we ended up having a photographer there, as well as reporters from *The Boston Globe* and local TV news outlets), and invited the local neighborhood to come shop and meet the local merchants and designers who were showcasing their exclusive items at the pop-up shop. Our goal was to position our pop-up as being more than just a combination of artisanal stores—we were intent on making it a destination. You should think similarly, as our best days surrounded those special events that we created.

Social media is also huge in helping to build awareness for your brand. Even if you have never used Twitter or Facebook, there are some simple things you can do to create an online presence and connect with your customers. First, create a website. It doesn't have to be fancy, and there are platforms like Wix.com that allow you to do it for free, but you need *something* that lets customers know you're there. What type of content should you have on your site? It can be as simple as your basic information (brand name, location of the pop-up shop, hours of operation, etc.), images of your products, or if you have the skills or know someone who does, you can create a more advanced site that enables customers to visualize the products you are selling (or food you are serving) at the pop-up, and perhaps even buy your products online through a payment portal such as PayPal. If you go the e-commerce route, it is preferable to use it more as a "teaser" or promotional tool to lure customers to your physical pop-up store, where you can meet them and have them check out your goods in person and have special features pointed out to them.

Even if you are not proficient in social media, adding notices in local newspapers (Patch.com is a great way to get word out there for free, as they are an online local publication that has a presence in many cities and towns throughout the country) about your pop-up shop or your website is a great way to build awareness. If you are familiar with Facebook and Twitter, these can be huge for the overall success of your pop-up. A Facebook page can enhance your connection with your customers, allowing you to post images, add updates, or interact directly with your fans. Twitter works a little differently. Your messages, called "Tweets," are confined to 140 characters or fewer, but if you can figure it out, it is the equivalent of speaking through a loudspeaker at the top of a mountain. The ability for friends and followers to re-tweet and "favorite" your tweets enables your message to spread fast, and it is the perfect tool for you to create an active customer base and brand loyalty. Setting up "business" Facebook and Twitter accounts is easy, free, and can be quite productive.

Outfitting the Space

Depending on the type of space in which you are opening your pop-up, there are several factors to keep in mind as you fill your space with furniture. If you are taking over a previously occupied space, you can ask whether the previous tenant will leave shelving, hanging racks, tables, or chairs for you to use for your pop-up. This will significantly decrease the amount you'll have to spend, and if you are a fashion designer or retailer, clothing racks and hangers will be your most essential expense.

If you will be opening in an empty, bare-bones space, ask for a floor plan before moving in. This way, you can easily decide where you will put tables, desks, shelving, and any other furniture that you need. Also, make sure to take pictures of the space as a shell so that, if you want to paint the walls, you'll be able to get a better sense of what colors will go well with the overall décor of the space if you have pictures to analyze.

In terms of how to actually obtain the furniture, I'd suggest you do an online search for furniture rental companies. Depending on the duration of your pop-up, it will be most cost-effective to rent anything you'll need, as opposed to buying. Rental companies will likely charge by the day, so in some cases, it actually might be worthwhile to buy. It really depends on the type of pop-up you're opening, the size of the space, and how long your pop-up will be open.

Expenses

Just like any business, you need to pay careful attention to expenses associated with your pop-up. While the temporary nature of pop-ups eliminates a lot of risk, it also leaves very little margin for error and requires careful planning to make sure you achieve your goals: to become a successful business and to make money.

No matter where you live or where your business will be located, rent, insurance, and permits/licenses are fixed expenses associated with almost every pop-up. Everything else—staffing, signs/banners, furniture/fixtures, promotion, advertising—can be customized or managed to fit within a specific budget. For example, let's create an expense report for a 30-day pop-up in New York City:

- *Rent:* $10,000 (a 2,500-square-foot space in Manhattan)
- *Insurance:* $500
- *Permits/Licenses:* $250
- *Staffing:* $7,200.00 for 8 (hours) x $10 (dollars/day) x 30 (days), x 3 (number of employees hired)
- *Furniture/Fixtures:* $2,500 (includes basic P.O.S. system, shelving, desks, other operational expenses)
- *Promotion:* $3,000 (includes grand opening event)
- *Signs:* $500 (can easily be printed at a FedEx office or another local sign maker)
- *Advertising:* $500
- *Total expenses for 30-day pop-up shop:* **$23,950**

This is a pretty extreme case for a 30-day pop-up, as New York City is among the most expensive for commercial leasing in the United States. However, it should give you a sense of what can be expected for a large-scale pop-up in a major city. In terms of revenue projections and break-even points, it's a matter of simple arithmetic based on your products, pricing, and so forth, but before you determine any of this information, it is important to figure out *what you will need to spend*, before determining *how much you want to make*.

When trying to determine your break-even point, it is *imperative* that you know your profit margins on the products you'll be selling. If your month's expenses are going to come to, say, $30,000, and your profit margins are 50 percent, you need to generate $60,000 in sales to break even. Know your break-even point.

Inventory/P.O.S. Systems

Choosing the right point-of-sale (P.O.S.) system is important. On average, businesses are charged between 2 and 4 percent on any purchases made, in store, via credit card (sometimes slightly higher for online purchases made via credit card). This can have an impact on the business, as that is money on each sale that is going out instead of coming in. Some systems work directly with iPads, while others, like the Square, can be attached to smartphones and used to track and transact with credit and debit cards. Handling cash is a little different, as that requires change and a more complex system than a simple Square or other credit card processor. There are now inexpensive cash registers that can be integrated into your P.O.S. system to make it all seamless, even handling inventory management in real time. If you are adept at creating and maintaining Excel spreadsheets, they can be very helpful in tracking sales, profitability, and inventory.

Staffing

The Most Important (and Overlooked) Aspect of a Pop-Up

THE POP-UP UNIVERSE is still vastly populated by artisanal merchants, be they aspiring chefs, designers, collectors, instructors, and makers of all kinds. They've been joined by well-known national brands, big-name celebrities, and the leading shopping malls.

All of the above have discovered pop-ups and how they can be used to generate income, promote upcoming events, and further enhance the reputations of brands and performers. Pop-ups entail several unique requirements—especially given their short durations—including finding the right venue; taking care of necessary insurance, permits, and logistics; arranging for point-of-sale and inventory tracking systems; and putting the word out and creating a "buzz" about the forthcoming pop-up. All of these requirements are dealt with elsewhere in this book.

But another necessity is also a prerequisite and is often the hardest to arrange, especially if you don't know where to look. That's the area of "staffing" the pop-up.

Pop-up staffing will generally fall into three broad categories—retail, dining, and events—categories that happen to coincide with how we divide up the pop-up directory on our website. While the thought might be "Hey, I only need a couple of people to work for a day or maybe a week, so I don't need to look for anyone with a lot of experience or relevant skills," that should *not* be your attitude when wanting to pull off a successful pop-up.

Staffing is the final piece of the pop-up puzzle. Once all of the planning is done, the venue is secured, the permits and setting are all set, and (in the case of pop-up restaurants or events), all of the tickets are sold, you are finally ready to open the doors and execute. The last thing you want is a poor performance. You want to succeed, to accomplish your goal(s), and to make people want to come to your next pop-up. To do that, even though your venue's look might be more rudimentary than the typical, polished retail or dining setting, you want your customer service to be impeccable.

If you are hosting a pop-up restaurant or supper club, you want the table to look beautiful and inviting. You want your customers to be greeted at the door, shown to their seats, and treated as though they are important guests. You want the food to be prepared to the highest order and service to be top-notch.

If you are hosting a pop-up retail event, you want your merchandise to be laid out well, pricing clearly noted, and to have retail help that has prior retail sales experience and familiarity with the product line being offered at the pop-up store.

If you are hosting a pop-up event, you want awesome brand ambassadors—a staff that is gracious, outgoing, conscientious, and there to make your customers happy.

When laid out this way, the task of finding proper help might sound a little daunting. Make no mistake, it is a challenge, and one you must win! The success of your pop-up will ultimately rest on your support staff. Employment agencies, public bulletin boards such as Craigslist or TaskRabbit, and, of course, your friends and family are some of the ways you might tackle this. But none of them are ideal sources for finding *temporary, yet professional* pop-up staffs.

PopUp Republic, as noted, is an end-to-end service provider to the pop-up industry. By end-to-end, we mean *start-to-finish*. We don't end our services at the point at which you open the pop-up for business. We are there to help all the way through the event. We can not only help organize and curate your pop-up, but we can also arrange for staff who have experience working at events such as the one you are planning. There are many sources of stress in launching a pop-up and the more responsibilities you can lay on the shoulders of others, the more you can focus in on areas of need. Having a staff that is largely self-managed is one major way to reduce a significant source of anxiety.

In addition to PopUp Republic, there are other reputable local and national staffing companies whose stables of on-call personnel can ably meet most, if not all, of your pop-up staffing needs. Especially if your plans call for a series of pop-ups in multiple locations, even those that might be taking place simultaneously or those that might be on a circuit of different venues in different states, having one company through which you can orchestrate the formulation and training of a capable staff for your pop-up will be invaluable. We can't emphasize that enough. Planning everything to the finest detail, but not having an experienced, capable staff to execute it at the same level, can undermine all of your hard work and otherwise well-deserved success.

Pop-Up Restaurants

For CHEFS, SOMMELIERS, food truck operators, permanent restaurants, or home cooks, opening a pop-up or creating a supper club provides an incredible opportunity to combine creativity and culinary proficiency. Some of the most incredible pop-ups that we have seen include restaurants of a variety of types, including Dinner in the Sky, a pop-up restaurant concept where award-winning chefs prepare gourmet meals for customers, with everyone being suspended via crane over some of the world's most iconic cities. Dinner in the Dark, a supper club where chefs prepare multi-course meals for blindfolded customers to create a whimsical, mysterious experience, is another unique, not-to-be-missed pop-up dining experience. Pop-up restaurants lend themselves to out-of-the-box creativity, so let your mind go wild—the setting can be as much a part of the pop-up dining experience as the food itself.

Ludo Lefebvre, dubbed the "Godfather of Pop-Ups," was one of the first chefs to create a roving pop-up dining concept. LudoBites launched in the Los Angeles market in the early 2000s as Chef Ludo was tired of the permanent restaurant scene and wanted an opportunity to be creative and work with various types of ingredients and menu items. He parlayed his pop-up success into an award-winning book and television gig on the hit ABC show *The Taste*. Pioneers like Ludo Lefebvre have moved the pop-up restaurant

Customers Participating in a Dinner in the Sky Pop-Up Dinner in Brussels, Belgium

concept forward and inspired chefs to leave high-paying, secure jobs as executive chefs at Michelin-award-winning restaurants to open roving pop-up dining concepts throughout the country. More and more, both professional and amateur chefs are realizing that pop-ups provide a realistic alternative to many of the challenges associated with the restaurant business and, since they are temporary, they allow these pop-ups to take place at interesting and creative locations throughout the country.

If you are someone whose association with eating out is on the consumption side rather than the production side—that is, if you are an eater, not a preparer—try to make it a point to visit a pop-up restaurant or join a supper club. It is a totally different dining experience, one in which you can interact with the chef and with other diners who are joining in the fun.

Seasonality

Seasonality for restaurants differs greatly than that of shops and provides more opportunities to change menus and introduce new concepts. Throughout the year we will see special pop-up restaurants with themed menu items for holidays such as New Years, Valentine's Day, Easter, Passover, July 4th, Halloween, Thanksgiving, and Christmas, as well as the time of year (Summer Solstice, Autumnal, Winter Wonderland, and many others). Chefs also create pop-ups based on pop culture; for instance, an incredibly popular dinner in London was a Game of Thrones pop-up concept, celebrating the show's premiere that occurred earlier this year. Themes like these are significant for pop-up restaurants. Chefs can create an entire concept based on their menus, allowing them to create a sense of urgency and excitement among their customers.

Unlike shops, pop-up restaurants don't necessarily benefit any more or less during the Christmas season holidays. In fact, it can be argued that they aren't as successful during those months, as a combination of the weather and spending priorities during that time of year can influence how much people can spend dining out. Usually, from New Years to Thanksgiving is the most popular time for pop-up dining events.

Types of Spaces

Creativity for pop-up restaurants also applies to the types of spaces that their organizers intend to utilize. For example, permanent restaurants have begun to rent out portions of their spaces to chefs to open up pop-up concepts. This is a variation of the store-within-a-store (restaurant-with-a-restaurant) concept described earlier; the benefit for restaurant owners is that it provides them with additional revenue opportunities (they can rent out their restaurants during off-hours, or even when they are closed). For pop-up organizers, a setup like this provides them with a state-of-the-art kitchen facility, existing foot traffic from the permanent restaurant's clientele, and a cost-effective solution to control rent and other expenses.

Personal kitchens are also becoming a popular venue for pop-up dining concepts. Sites like Kitchensurfing, Meal Sharing, and EatWith are actually built on this model. They are online directories full of private chefs, caterers, or home cooks who are creating private, intimate dining experiences. On these sites, you can purchase tickets and attend one of these unique events. These locations allow chefs to experiment with their creativity within the comforts of a personal residence, while monetizing an existing space (if you're a decent cook, and if you have room in your kitchen, why not sell tickets to the event and invite people to your personal supper club or pop-up dinner?). Furthermore, the expenses associated with a setup like this are significantly minimized; in fact, this model provides the highest profit margin of perhaps any other. By avoiding rent, insurance, furniture/fixtures, and building/business permits, the only fixed costs associated with operating a pop-up held in a private home would be for food and promotion. Plus, free online ticketing sites like Eventbrite.com allow you to sell tickets to your event, track orders, and interact directly with customers. Of course, PopUp Republic is probably your best option to connect directly with potential fans, as it can specifically target the customers you are trying to attract.

Licenses, Permits, and Insurance

Whatever type of space you choose for your pop-up restaurant or dining concept, a number of regulations may or may not apply, depending on your local ordinances. It is advised that you consult your local government's website, or contact a local official.

Furniture and Fixtures (Dependent on Type of Restaurant)

The cost of furnishing your pop-up restaurant has the potential to be significantly less (or significantly more) than for furnishing a pop-up shop. If you were to open a pop-up dining concept in an existing restaurant, you're likely to be able to use the existing furniture in that restaurant (the owners of the restaurant might add that as a cost associated with rent, but it should be less than it would be to rent new furniture from a rental company).

If you are going the commercial space route, your most expensive purchase would be to buy kitchen equipment that meets the standards associated with the local Board of Health, and your own standards to execute your dining concept effectively. That is why it is so important to find a vacant commercial space that has kitchen equipment built in. Depending on how familiar you are with the location in which you are opening your pop-up, this should be fairly easy to find. Any old restaurant or commissary space will do, or a public space that has available kitchen facilities. Given the temporary nature of pop-ups, it is not very cost-effective and does not make a lot of sense to commit to a large buildout or allocate a significant portion of your budget toward designing and building a new kitchen.

Using a personal residence for your pop-up could be the most cost-effective solution, as the space likely already has the kitchen, cooking equipment, utensils, tables, and chairs that you will need to run a successful event.

Food Trucks

When we first started our company, one of the first decisions that we made seems a bit silly, but ultimately played a major factor in determining our perspective of the pop-up industry: Can food trucks be considered pop-ups?

As mentioned, pop-ups are temporary, one-off events that provide a fear-of-missing-out experience for customers. They are here today, gone tomorrow, and create a sense of urgency that is not found in any other retail or dining experience.

Food trucks offer much of the same—food that you can't get anywhere, passion and love that is not typically found in permanent restaurants, and creativity that is limitless. However, many of the food trucks we have worked with open every day, in various locations around towns and cities nationwide. Can something that is open every day, but will often appear in a different location, be considered a pop-up? Our answer is "yes."

The food truck dates back to the 1800s, when Texas-based cattle rancher Charles Goodnight outfitted an old chuck wagon with shelving, drawers, kitchenware, and foods such as beans, coffee, and bacon, and followed various trails that led him to markets in the Northern and Eastern United States. Nowdays, mobile dining innovators such as Los Angeles–based Roy Choi use food trucks as creative dining concepts, creating multi-million-dollar businesses out of these roving restaurants.

Rules and Regulations

The rules and regulations associated with operating a food truck are similar to those of a pop-up restaurant. Since they often contain fully equipped kitchens, a health department inspection is needed to maintain food quality and safety.

Technically, it is illegal to park a vehicle of any kind on city streets and sell products from it without appropriate paperwork. Luckily, several cities and towns throughout the country have developed protocols to obtain the proper licenses needed to legally operate a food truck. Additionally, some cities have even adopted legal food truck zones, where trucks can line up and serve food to hungry customers in busy metropolitan areas.

Promotion

The biggest challenge for food trucks is also the biggest benefit. Unlike traditional pop-up restaurants, food trucks can aggressively pursue customers by rolling up to large masses of people at events, office parks, concerts, or on busy streets. This provides an excellent opportunity to maximize foot traffic without much expense or effort. On the other hand, it's not always easy to find the right location, and, similarly, success can be difficult if you are overwhelmed with customers or do not have enough food to serve large crowds.

Setting a "game plan" each day is essential for a food truck, as they should know where they are going to go and how much food is required. Other tools, such as social media sites like Twitter, Instagram, and Pinterest, websites like roaminghunger.com, and the media can be helpful to promote your truck and attract customers.

Riding Solo vs. Blending In

Customers love variety. If they see three food trucks lined up side-by-side, they are more likely to make a purchase from all three trucks than if they saw just one truck standing by itself. It's almost the principle of supply and demand, but in reverse: since consumers have so many dining options, food trucks can create a sense of urgency by partnering with other trucks to open in the same location during the same time period.

Similarly, both consumers and food trucks are equally attracted to organized food truck festivals. These types of events allow customers to try a "taste" of the offerings served from a variety of different trucks, while it provides the truck operators with exposure to a larger group of customers and potentially more customers than if they were in a single location on a given afternoon.

Accounting for the Weather

Mother nature is the single biggest factor that can determine the success or failure of a food truck. It's common sense—if it's nice out, more people are outside, which means more customers will visit the truck, which results in higher revenue numbers. If there is bad weather, there is less chance of significant foot traffic, smaller revenue numbers, but a higher operating cost (operating costs per diner decrease the more customers who are served, since more revenue is generated).

That is why permanent restaurants often have food trucks of their own. They realize that they can attract new customers from other areas of the city or town in which they are located, but also pick and choose which dates their trucks are open based on the weather. Using a truck to supplement an existing business is a great way to enhance your brand and maintain customer loyalty.

The Yum Dum Food Truck Serves Hungry Customers in Downtown Chicago

Interview with Jeff Wang, Owner/Operator of Yum Dum Food Truck in Chicago, Illinois

THE YUM DUM truck can be found on Twitter at @YumDumTruck, and on Facebook at www.facebook.com/yumdumtruck. Customers can taste the delicious offerings from Jeff and his crew, including "Kimcheesy Rice Balls," "Sriracha Pecan Browniez," and "Baowiches," at various locations throughout Chicago.

> **Q: What is your background and what led you to open a food truck?**
>
> *I went to the University of Illinois and studied economics. Not exactly your typical path to owning a food truck. After graduating, I did what most 20-something college grads do and worked in corporate America. However, sitting in front of a computer for 8 plus hours per day wasn't my idea of how I wanted to spend the rest of his life. So I left my finance job and pursued my passion for food.*
>
> *I grew up around food since my parents came over to America and opened Chinese restaurants. I always knew I'd eventually find*
>
> (continued)

(*continued*)

my way back to the kitchen; I just never knew it would be in a truck.

The idea for a food truck came to me when I was in Taiwan at a night market and really developed my love for street food. I wanted to bring the amazing street food that my parents grew up eating and cooked for us back to Chicago, and a food truck seemed to best articulate my message.

Q: What are the main reasons you think food trucks have become so popular so quickly?

I think the quality of food has become the driving factor for the popularity of food trucks. There is so much amazing food you can get from trucks and no longer just from high-end, expensive restaurants. It starts with guys like Roy Choi (Kogi) in LA and Paul Qui (ESK) in Austin, who have taken the food truck game to a whole new level.

But credit should also be given to the consumers, too, because they are what drive our business. There are so many people today who love finding food trucks and love the experience and interaction. We're not stationary and move around so it's exciting when you see your favorite truck in your neighborhood. It's a lot of fun for the customers and us too!

Q: Are food truck owners largely "foodies," or are they drawn to it by the business potential they see?

I think a little bit of both. Food truck owners are devoted to their craft. There's nothing better than seeing the happiness our food brings to people. It's all about sharing my culture and childhood through my food, and that's why I opened the truck, not for the money. We work long hours and sacrifice a lot for our trucks, sometimes for no money at all. However, I'd be lying if I said I wasn't also driven by the business potential of a great food truck. I don't mean monetary, but the opportunities of running a great truck are endless. I want to be the best at what I do, and that *includes being the best food trucker I can be. I want people to recognize the truck and love our food, and the rest will fall into place.*

Q: How can the food truck business be scaled? Own a lot of food trucks throughout the city? Open pop-up restaurants as a next step? Expand to other cities?

That's what I love about the food truck business; there are so many opportunities for expansion. Many food truck operators use their success to open a brick-and-mortar restaurant. You already have a following, so this seems to be the natural next step. I think it's always a dream to open up your own shop and run the truck out of there. However, I love just being a food truck. It's so much fun and much less stress. There is so much less risk and fewer overhead costs compared to a brick and mortar. Sometimes opening more trucks is just more economical. It'll definitely add to your outreach and build your customer base. Perhaps one of these new trucks will be in another city. I would love to make Yum Dum into a national brand, but Rome wasn't built in one day.

Q: Chicago is already getting a reputation for its outstanding food truck scene. Is there anything you can identify about Chicago that makes it so receptive to food trucks?

Chicago is the greatest culinary city in the world, but we are playing catch up on the food truck scene. We are starting to embrace all the great food trucks of our city. There are so many people looking for great food in our city, and this isn't limited to just the restaurants. Nothing beats summertime in Chicago, and there's always a food truck nearby. There's a lot of exciting things happening for our industry here!

Q: How tough has it been regulatory-wise?

There's a lot of rules and regulations, but nothing impossible. The city has been a lot more receptive of food trucks and has been

(continued)

(continued)

doing great things to streamline the process and getting more, great trucks out on the road. My biggest wish is for more legal truck stands around Chicago, which would make our lives a whole lot easier.

Q: How much capital do you need to start a food truck?

This varies with every food truck and every concept. It's all based on what type of food you'll be cooking, what type of equipment you'll need, and what style of truck you want to build.

Fashion Trucks

You HEAR ABOUT it, you read about it, you see it everywhere. This is the Era of Mobile. Smartphones are everywhere, seemingly glued as an appendage to people's ears. Stand in a crowd and, almost invariably, you will see someone with head bowed, seemingly deep in prayer, when actually he or she is merely reading the latest text that was telecommunicated to the little electronic box he is holding in his hands.

But this "Era of Mobile" has started to take on a secondary meaning as well. Mobile is beginning to refer to the method by which retailers meet face-to-face with prospective customers. There is online, represented by the mass of retailers who sell their products on the web. There is offline, personified by brick-and-mortar stores and malls. And now there is mobile, which is being led by food trucks.

The food truck sector is still in its early stages. The industry is just starting. Entrepreneurs are beginning to recognize the potential and low cost of entry. The public is just now recognizing that some of the most delicious food in the neighborhood at lunchtime is literally just around the corner. Regulators are salivating not only at the prospect at eating at one of these roving restaurants, but also at the new area in which they can construct a web of rules and licenses—and taxes—that will dramatically impact the speed in which this retail segment will take hold. It *will* happen, as public appetite for the convenience and culinary talents of the food truck impresarios is already making clear. But the regulators will be there to ensure that all interests are safeguarded, including public health factors and protective covenants to benefit local brick-and-mortar merchants, and this tends to move slowly.

Besides those who are direct stakeholders in the growth of the food truck industry—the truck owners, the nearby restaurants, the lunchtime crowd, the regulators—there is also an interested group of spectators, namely, apparel designers and retailers. Aspiring designers and clothing retailers face many of the same obstacles that entrepreneurial food vendors do, with the biggest one being the commitment that is required to go into business. This commitment takes many forms.

There is the financial commitment. As with a brick-and-mortar restaurant, the cost to open a store is monumental, often well into six figures. This cost is also fraught with financial risks. One often has to enter into a multi-year lease, usually as long as five or ten years. There is a significant buildout involved that requires considerable up-front expenditures. Few people have socked away enough savings to pay for all these costs, so—in most cases—one has to borrow money from a bank—large sums that have to be paid back monthly, with interest.

There is the time commitment. A shop owner has to post her hours and then make sure the store is open during those hours. Quite often, this includes specific hours and days that are acknowledged as being low periods for shoppers to patronize the stores or dine at the restaurant. Still, it is too difficult to open and close permanent physical stores for certain periods of the day and week. Time commitment includes another element; it often translates into an owner having to give up another job in order to minister to her brick-and-mortar store, to which she has made a major financial commitment.

Those who have always had an eye and a passion for the fashion industry, much in the same way as those who have longed to enter the food industry, have been scared off by such forbidding cost and time commitments. But they have been watching what has been going on with the food industry—and been inspired. If food can be sold from roaming purveyors, why not apparel?

Thus has emerged a new entrant in mobile commerce—the fashion truck. For an even lower cost to enter than a food truck, *fashionistas* are able to enter a world they are passionate about, usually spending in the five figures to procure and outfit a truck and build an initial inventory. Typically, additional operating costs include about $1,000 a month for gas, maintenance, and parking, and another $100 to $200 for various space rental fees. As a category, fashion trucks began their ascent in 2010, expanding very rapidly in the past couple of years. There already exists a nascent infrastructure to support this burgeoning business sector.

The American Mobile Retail Association (AMRA) defines itself as "a growing group of mobile retailers in the U.S. working in collaboration with the same goal—to bring recognition and growth to the innovative industry of mobile boutiques and services." Last year, AMRA estimated that there were about 500 fashion trucks operating in all 50 states.

The fashion truck industry faces far fewer legal restrictions than the food truck industry does. Mostly, this relates to the fact that food trucks must comply with strict local food preparation ordinances. One doesn't become sick by wearing a new scarf or outfit.

But the fashion truck industry also doesn't have a built-in local constituency. A fashion truck can't simply park a truck between the hours of noon and 2 p.m. and expect a hungry crowd of office workers to stream out of nearby office buildings in search of food and get in line to purchase their offerings.

Rather, fashion truck owners, for the time being at least, have to set up schedules in advance of where their trucks will appear, based on the schedules of fairs and festivals and private events that are arranged by third parties. Flea markets, one-day expos, private and block parties, and holiday festivals are the temporary venues at which fashion trucks now open for business. Fortunately, these events tend to be open during times and days when the truck operators themselves are most available to park and vend—largely weekends and holidays—although "serious" fashion truck merchants, such as Laura Layton of Tin Lizzy Mobile Boutique, find ways to be open throughout the week.

Laura's Tin Lizzy Mobile Boutique

As an example, here is a copy of Tin Lizzy's initial summer 2015 schedule, one to which she continued to add events as weeks went on:

June

- June 17th–21st: Firefly Music Festival's Northeast Hub, Dover, DE
- June 26th–28th: Big Barrel Country Music Festival, Dover, DE

July

- July 2nd: First Thursday Concert in the Park at Canton Waterfront Park, Baltimore, MD
- July 8th: Truck PopUp at Whole Foods Market in Columbia, MD
- July 15th: PopUp at Bethesda Farm Women's Coop, 7155 Wisconsin Ave., Bethesda, MD
- July 17th: Truck PopUp at Whole Foods Market in Columbia, MD, 10 am to 6 pm

- July 18th & 19th: Fashion, Food & Film at Baltimore ArtScape, 1812 N. Charles St., Baltimore, MD
- July 22nd: PopUp at Bethesda Farm Women's Coop, 7155 Wisconsin Ave., Bethesda, MD
- July 24th: Fashion Truck Friday in Rosslyn, Arlington, VA, Plaza on 19th, 10 am–2 pm

August

- August 6th: First Thursday Concert in the Park at Canton Waterfront Park, Baltimore, MD
- August 15th: Hot August Music Festival, Oregon Ridge Park, Cockeysville, MD
- August 21st: The Gathering at Baltimore Museum of Industry, Baltimore, MD
- August 28th: Fashion Truck Friday in Rosslyn, Arlington, VA, 1700 block of Lynn St.

Interview with Laura Layton, Owner of Tin Lizzy Mobile Boutique

TIN LIZZY IS a 1997 Grumman Step Van given a new life as a traveling shop specializing in fair trade, ethically and locally made apparel, accessories and gifts. Tin Lizzy travels the Mid-Atlantic region, setting up shop at festivals, markets, on the side of the road, and wherever customers want to shop.

Tin Lizzy is owned and operated by small business lover, Laura Layton. Laura is passionate about knowing where goods come from, telling the stories behind the merchandise she sells, and creating unique shopping experiences.

Q: Did you have a background in retail and/or fashion?

Yes. I graduated from the University of Delaware with a degree in fashion merchandising and leadership. I always had dreams of opening my own boutique and being a small business owner. I have worked various retail jobs from a young age, but after college I started working for fair trade retailers and non-profits because

(continued)

(continued)

I realized that's the type of retail I was most interested in. While I felt as prepared as I could be to open my business, there are so many things you just have to learn along the way.

Q: How did you end up taking the route you chose, namely, a fashion truck? When did it first start? How much time do you spend on the business?

I originally wrote a business plan for a brick-and-mortar boutique with the same concept as my truck—all fair trade, ethically made goods—but I had a lot of reservations. A long-term lease frightened me. I wanted the smallest possible space and I ideally wanted to own that space. I ultimately decided to open the truck to save money on startup costs, but I love it for so many reasons now, mainly because of its versatility. I am able to travel all over the state, trying out different cities and towns, setting up shop at wine festivals, street fairs, operating with permits similar to a food truck, doing private parties. There are so many options available to me. I bought my truck in January of 2014 and launched the following April.

I spend a lot of time on my business, and when I'm not physically spending time in the truck or in front of the computer, I'm usually thinking about it in some form or another. I typically have the truck on the road five days a week and need at least one full day for admin work. I spend a lot of time booking up my schedule, making sure the truck is adequately stocked with merchandise, and adding inventory to my online shop.

Q: How's it going? Is it getting easier? What's been the most difficult part? The most fulfilling? Are things going pretty much as planned and expected?

Things are going so well! I am on track to increase my annual sales by 100 percent this year. I would not say it's getting easier, but I would says it's getting more fun! As I get busier I'm finding it more difficult to keep up with the day-to-day tasks and be able to focus on growing my business. The more I learn and experience, the more I want to grow my business but so far, I am only one person. Being only one person, at times it can feel overwhelming, and I'd say that's the most difficult part. You're in charge of making every decision, and you're 100 percent responsible for failures and successes. The most fulfilling part of owning this business is working for myself and being able to do it full time. I can't remember the last time I dreaded a Monday or didn't want to go to work. I truly love what I do, and I know that my customers can see that as well.

One unexpected thing I've encountered since opening this business is all of the wonderful relationships I have formed with other small business owners in my community. I feel so supported and inspired by other like-minded individuals I have met through Tin Lizzy, and it has been so rewarding to be a part of a community of creative individuals working hard to grow their businesses together.

Q: What are the ultimate goals and wishes for Tin Lizzy?

I just want to keep growing Tin Lizzy in whatever way makes the most sense for my brand. I am really interested to see what happens in the next few years in the mobile retail world, and I plan to keep the truck on the road for as long as it makes sense. If the mobile retail industry continues to grow as it has, I would like to have multiple trucks on the road in the next three to five years. One of my main goals for 2015 was to grow my online shop, and that goal will probably carry on into 2016. I also want to start experimenting with brick-and-mortar pop-up shops and events this winter and give the truck a rest throughout the winter months.

Pop-Up Spaces

Summary

Three years ago, when the number of pop-ups first began to dramatically increase in the United States, they typically opened in vacant storefronts or empty restaurants located on city streets or in suburban strip malls throughout the country. Nowadays, while pop-ups at these venues are still popular, we are seeing them also open in public spaces (gardens, churches, even parking lots), within existing businesses (stores-within-stores, restaurants-within-restaurants), personal residences (garages, driveways, kitchens), on mountain tops, underwater, in cemeteries, on Ferris wheels, or even being hoisted by construction equipment (as per the aforementioned Dinner in the Sky, a pop-up dining concept where patrons are suspended in the air via a crane). Clearly, as people are experimenting with creative, one-of-a-kind pop-up concepts, they are looking for equivalent spaces that provide a whimsical, incredible setting for their events.

Benefits/Costs

Individual landlords, property management companies, real estate agents, and even shopping malls are embracing the concept of pop-ups for a variety of reasons. When we first launched PopUp

Republic in 2012, landlords we approached were often reluctant to use our service because they did not immediately understand how and why pop-ups would benefit them. Landlords have always been in search of permanent tenants, and even to this day there are many empty spaces throughout the City of Chicago, where PopUp Republic is headquartered, that would be perfect locations for pop-ups but are instead sitting empty.

As pop-ups have gained a larger following over the last couple of years, landlords have started to realize that they are great ways to fill vacancies on a temporary basis—after all, some rent is better than no rent, and temporary pop-up tenants could even sign long-term leases if they end up having success during the time in which their pop-up is open. As municipalities have embraced pop-ups, they have also encouraged landlords to become more accepting of them, as it's been proven that pop-ups are a great mechanism to boost economies and revitalize urban areas.

For pop-up merchants, whether they are still developing a name or are established brands, appearing in an upscale mall presents an opportunity to be in a high-trafficked location, become associated with other big-name brands, and position a pop-up as a destination for consumers. Malls are particularly perfect locations for large brands to start a pop-up, as they often have experiential spaces that are perfectly designed to create an enhanced discovery experience for customers. Online retailers can utilize pop-ups to create a "touch-and-feel" experience for their customers, to promote a new product line, or to tap into a new market. The new omnichannel marketing trend is very compatible with both pop-ups and major malls, especially if the brand wants to gain exposure in multiple cities.

Expectations as a Landlord

The most important trait that any good landlord has is to be there for tenants. The best tenant/landlord relationships we have seen exist when there are clear guidelines that the tenant has to abide by, while the landlord develops a contract that is fair for both sides.

Often, spaces are expected to come "as-is," and the outfitting/ construction of the space is paid for by the tenant, subject to the agreement of the landlord or property owner. A standard lease is drafted (consult local small business associations/chambers of commerce, or other landlords, for sample leases). They are also available via a simple online search) and agreed to between the lessor (landlord) and lessee (tenant). In some cases, a license or other contractual arrangement other than a real estate lease is preferable for both sides, as leases can entail a host of other legal stipulations that can otherwise be avoided.

As a landlord, you are also expected to establish protocols regarding the day-to-day maintenance of the space. Depending on the nature of the circumstance, this can include minor tasks such as changing light bulbs, to fixing refrigerators or dishwashers, to rebuilding a space after a fire. It is advised that you have an insurance policy on your space, in case of emergency.

Becoming a Pop-Up Landlord

The emergence of the pop-up movement as an economic force isn't limited to the sales generated by the pop-ups themselves. Pop-ups have also become instrumental in creating new sources of income for property owners—and even some property lessees—and that applies to virtually any sort of real estate one can think of!

Pop-ups have made landlords think unconventionally about when and how their properties could be used for revenue generation. Traditional uses—those things we do because, well, "that's how we always do it"—are being given a second look, and real estate owners are finding new opportunities to add incremental income by incorporating pop-ups into their business models.

Stores-Within-Stores and Restaurants-Within-Restaurants

While a wide assortment of settings can be good locations for pop-ups, there is one category we believe is at the very top of the pyramid—stores-within-stores and restaurants-within-restaurants. These types of arrangements typically save both the pop-up host and the permanent proprietor lots of time and money, creating win-win situations from both perspectives.

Let's say a shopkeeper or a restaurant operator enters into a typical long-term lease of her storefront—say, a five-year term. During that 60-month lease, on the first day of each and every month, the shopkeeper starts off in a deep hole. The entire month's rent is due, a fixed cost that is the same irrespective of how many hours the store is actually open and how much business volume is generated that month. Add other overhead costs to that, such as staffing, utilities, insurance, etc.—and the hole from which the operator must dig out gets mighty deep very, very quickly.

Overhead costs—the basic costs to open the doors and operate the business regardless of how much income there is—are the bane of every store or restaurant operator—really, of every type of business. They represent the fixed numerator over an as-yet-to-be-known denominator of the risk/reward ratio. You know how much money you will have at risk that month . . . but you have no idea how much revenue there will be to offset those costs. Not an ideal position to be in, and one every business should be looking to ameliorate to the greatest extent possible.

Let's illustrate: Please meet Violet, a fictional boutique owner. Violet, an acknowledged "green thumb" with a flair for decoration, has been growing and designing flower arrangements for friends for many years. She was always encouraged to do it as a business, and this year she finally took the plunge, taking immense pride as she put up a shingle for Violet's Florals, Ltd., and hung a hopeful "Open for Business" sign in the window—a day she will never forget.

Even with all of her percolating excitement, Violet knew that, especially at the outset of her new enterprise, she would have to watch every nickel, and she did just that. However, not even taking into account the money she borrowed for fixtures and decorations to adorn her 1,500-square-foot flower boutique—money she had to pay back in monthly installments—Violet had a "nut" of some $6,000 a month. At a relatively modest $20 per square foot, her rent, due on the first of every month, was $2,500 ($30,000 a year). Her utilities, a relatively high number because of a need to keep some of her flowers under refrigeration, came to $800 a month. Violet hired a sales clerk to help her manage the business, an expense that came to $1,800. Insurance, permits, supplies, and other incidentals came to $900. This all came to a total fixed cost of $6,000—before she made a single sale and before she took out any money for herself.

The flower business allows for some pretty attractive margins, with Violet's retail prices reflecting a gross profit margin of some 67 percent. Not a bad variable cost scenario to deal with, indeed! But with a monthly fixed expense of $6,000, and a cost of goods equaling 33 percent of sales, that means that Violet's break even each month—before she could pay herself her first dime—was $9,000. Anything less than that meant that Violet was losing money.

A natively smart business woman, Violet decided upon a strategy that could potentially increase the flow of foot traffic into her store and thus generate more sales, while at the same time reduce her monthly expenses and thereby lower her break-even point. An important note to keep in mind: For every $1.00 in sales that Violet generated, she kept 67 cents (her profit margin). But for every $1.00 in reduced expenses, she benefitted from the full $1.00. So in calculating how she could make ends meet each month, Violet correctly figured that she could reach profitability faster for every dollar not spent than she would for every dollar in sales she generated.

Most entrepreneurs don't think that way. They are optimists. They believe in their ability to build sales quickly and thus to turn a profit. They become liberal, even a little spendthrift, putting their focus on the upside of their fledgling venture—sales and profits—rather than the downside—expenses and losses. But soon reality sets in. Violet knew she couldn't avoid that first-of-the-month pressure entirely, but she sure was determined to reduce it as much as she could.

So what did Violet do? In one corner of her store, she segregated 300 square feet of space, figuring that 1,200 square feet was sufficient for her own needs. She put an ad in the paper, saying she would sub-lease space in her flower shop to a suitable pop-up for $1,000 a month rent. Violet received a reply from a merchant who made fragrant, handmade soaps. Violet decided that could be a perfect fit. Great fragrances to complement the aromas of her flowers, what was likely to be added incremental foot traffic, no direct competition. A three-month sublease was agreed to between Violet and the pop-up soap maker.

For the pop-up, it was a good deal. No insurance, no utilities, no long-term commitment, no buildout, and the benefit of the foot traffic that the flower shop would be generating. For Violet, it was also a good deal. By reducing her rent to $1,500 a month, her fixed expenses would be reduced to $5,000. With profit margins at 67 percent, she reduced her break-even to $7,500 a month. Plus, she had the benefit of the additional foot traffic that the soap maker would attract.

This sort of store-within-a-store concept doesn't just create a win-win at the small, indie boutique level. Nordstrom and Target, to name two big brand stores, have developed a history of curating pop-up shops within their stores as a means to bring in new customers, generate a bigger "per ticket" spend, and benefit economically from their temporary tenants. This formula is being replicated more and more among well-known retailers.

And it works even better when it comes to restaurants-within-restaurants, for a number of important reasons:

First, most restaurants tend to operate during shortened daytime hours. A restaurant that specializes in dinner rarely is open for breakfast and lunch as well. Conversely, a restaurant that is open for breakfast and lunch is often closed for dinner. Additionally, many restaurants are closed one to two days a week—for example, a restaurant that caters to the daytime office crowd is often closed over weekends. Many restaurants that specialize in dinner are closed on Mondays, customarily the slowest day of the week for dining out. And many restaurants close by no later than 10 p.m.

But the clock keeps ticking when it comes to the restaurateur's fixed costs, whether the restaurant is open or closed. Each second of the day costs the proprietor rent, insurance, license fees, and other attendant costs.

Second, from the perspective of the pop-up restaurant merchant, there are more complexities for an entrepreneur who is looking to host a pop-up restaurant than for one wanting to open a pop-up store. A pop-up dining host needs kitchen prep facilities and cooking equipment. He needs tables, chairs, linens, even dishes and flatware. Perhaps most challenging of all, he needs to have a space that is compliant with local health department ordinances.

Challenges from two opposite perspectives, but that can be met by a restaurant-within-a-restaurant arrangement.

Empty Storefronts

Empty storefronts stick out like sore thumbs. You can have nine stores occupied, but having just one vacant raises questions about the viability of a neighborhood. Landlords hate them, for obvious reasons.

But if you are looking for a space in which to open a pop-up shop or pop-up restaurant, they are golden, the quintessential space in which to operate a pop-up. A pop-up is not expected to engage in a massive buildout or to install fancy signage. Shoppers recognize—even expect—that a pop-up shop is there temporarily, and the rudimentary setting somehow adds to the experience. This broadens the universe of prospective tenants for the property owner and increases the appeal of the empty storefronts.

That said, there has been a recent change in the quality of stores being made available for short-term pop-ups. Shopping malls, even the upscale ones, had shied away from making their vacant shops available for pop-ups. It wasn't so much any stigma that they attached to the pop-up concept, although perhaps there was a small fear that an impression might be given that the mall couldn't attract permanent tenants. Rather, the mall operators clung to the notion that they are different from one-off commercial property owners and were committed to recruiting only long-term lessees.

With the dangerous competition that malls were facing from online retail, which resulted in a drop in shopper visitations in many shopping centers because people were able to buy their favorite products online and have them shipped and delivered overnight in some cases, malls were frantically looking for ways to counter this encroachment on their sacred turf.

Fortunately for them, a new realization came to the e-commerce community—they were experiencing a significant problem. There were too many customer returns, a result of the inability of the customer to see, touch, and try on items they bought until they were delivered to their homes. A large majority of online consumers have said that they have returned items to their online retailers from whom they bought items—sometimes on a regular basis.

Online retailers chose to turn to their competition—the shopping malls—and, rather than compete with them, they worked with them. This has clearly helped the mall owner/operators. Shopping centers now are very amenable to hosting pop-up shops, especially from the big brands and online retailers, but even from the local artisanal and boutique community, as this brings freshness and exclusivity to the mall offerings, which in turn brings in foot traffic.

Interview with Aaron Gadiel, Shopping Center Executive

AARON GADIEL HAS spent more than 20 years in commercial real estate. He has developed and implemented many types of pop-up concepts, primarily as a means to position his properties as a "destination" among consumers. He has also worked with several large brands that have created activation experiences for customers.

Q: What is your background?

Real estate professional for the past 20 years. Got my start doing residential appraisals, moved to brokerage, then shopping center development. In my "spare time," I've been an amateur promoter for the last 25 years, producing everything from concerts, movie screenings, antique markets, and food festivals. My work mantra had always been: "Real estate is how I feed my family, and being a promoter is how I feed my soul." Feel like I've been able to marry the two with my work on the marketing side of the real estate world. (continued)

(*continued*)

Q: **When did you first hear about pop-ups, and when did you start implementing them in your mall?**

My first exposure to pop-up stores was through a seasonal temporary lease I did in 2005. It was a Halloween costume store that only wanted to be open from September 1 through November 1. I remember thinking to myself at the time, "great business model!" In 2008, when the retail world fell off a cliff, I started to look at these temporary leasing opportunities, or "pop-up stores," as a way to fill vacant space at a shopping center I was leasing. Pop-up stores quite literally might've saved our shopping center through a very difficult time period. I've been focusing on these types of opportunities ever since.

Q: **Why have you used pop-ups? What advantages do they provide property managers? When a pop-up opens at one of your malls, how do the permanent stores feel about having a temporary "neighbor"?**

Pop-up stores achieve several different objectives. The most obvious is that they fill vacant space and provide ancillary income to landlords until the space can be permanently leased. Pop-up stores also create a unique shopping experience consumers cannot find anywhere else. This is especially critical as shopping centers seek to differentiate themselves from the competitors. Permanent tenants are typically fine with pop-up stores, as they would much rather see activity in a space than it sit dark and vacant. The real win-win opportunity is when you can find the right kind of pop-up store, which complements or even adds to the overall merchandising mix of a center. Everyone is successful, and it's the best opportunity for a pop-up store to become a permanent tenant.

Q: How have pop-ups contributed to the revitalization of some of your properties?

Pop-up stores have been a key element to the revitalization and ongoing leasing efforts, for many reasons, including: They provide activity and life in storefronts that would otherwise be vacant; show progress and ongoing changes to an otherwise stale environment; and incubate new retail concept ideas or provide a brick-and-mortar presence to Internet companies, all of which can lead to permanent tenancy.

Farmers Markets

THESE MAKESHIFT MARKETS make for an inviting space in which to exhibit and sell goods, especially on a part-time or temporary basis. Costs are drastically reduced—some spaces can be rented for under $50 a day or as a percentage of sales—and there is built-in shopper foot traffic, as these settings themselves are considered destinations and events with time sensitivities, since many are open only once a week or for a short duration.

Farmers markets, flea markets, and art/craft fairs are also perfect for "one item" sales. If you wrote a book, or you sell pickles, you probably would not be well-served to open a store, even a pop-up store, selling just one title or selling only pickles (even if your product lines include different kinds of pickles). But you might have the most popular booth at a temporary market where shoppers are looking for curiosities or hard-to-find, locally created products.

Public Spaces

Shopping malls are now capitalizing on another new realization—they are sitting on acres of land that are producing no income. The common areas inside the mall might look nice, and the parking lots might accommodate the needs of shoppers, but they produce no revenue and provide a fair amount of upkeep.

But no longer. Now, shopping centers and big box stores are looking at their common areas as spaces from which to generate incremental income. They have become the home to food truck festivals, food crawls, farmers and flea markets, and other public events that not only draw crowds, but also generate revenue.

In addition to these large private commercial properties, public spaces and non-traditional private spaces are joining the crowd. Houses of worship, which sometimes are in use only a few hours a week, have come to understand that they have commercial-level kitchens that are certified by the local health departments and areas both inside and outside that can accommodate pop-up gatherings. Parking lots, public parks, and even cemeteries have become settings for pop-up events, generating much-needed cash from otherwise underutilized assets, namely, their properties. This is a great opportunity for pop-up organizers to host their events in suitable, if non-traditional venues.

Matchmaking

If you are ready to take the plunge and become a pop-up landlord, if just on a trial basis, it is becoming easier to find a match. Service providers are stepping into the breach to help pair prospective spaces with prospective pop-up tenants. PopUp Insider and Storefront are two such enterprises in the United States, along with our favorite—PopUp Republic. By providing end-to-end services for pop-up merchants, landlords, mall operators, and pop-up customers, PopUp Republic is connected to all of the major players, which gives us a unique perch to help match properties with vendors and vice versa.

Flea Markets

FLEA MARKETS ARE big business. You may not think of them as such, but according to the National Flea Market Association (NFMA), there are over 1,100 flea markets that occur in the United States each year, with 2.25 million vendors generating over $30 billion in sales annually.

This gigantic turnover takes place for several reasons. For one thing, they can open both indoors and outdoors. They might be held in a school cafeteria or gym, or they might be held on a ball field or in a parking lot. They might even be held on cordoned-off city streets. Thus, you can almost always find a flea market going on somewhere nearby.

There is also an almost limitless array of items sold at flea markets. Antiques—bric-a-brac—unique handmade products—old clothes—unwanted household items—expensive items typically deeply discounted—there is almost no end.

A hodgepodge of time durations also contributes to the plethora of flea markets that take place at any given time. Flea markets can be held year-round, such as Chelsea Market in New York City, which seems to always be teeming with visitors. They might be seasonal or monthly, on weekends or daily, ongoing or one-off.

No matter where, how often, how long, and what type of products are being sold, the formats of flea markets are generally the same: There is a marketplace set up, and vendors are able to rent booths within the market from which to sell their goods. Booth and set-up fees are so variable, from as low as $5 a day to well over $500 a month, that they are hardly worth mentioning. But it seems that no matter the type, cost, time span, and setting, vendors at flea markets always seem to be having a lot of fun.

By and large, vendors should be able to walk away at the conclusion of the day with more money than when they came in. One can sell almost anything at a flea market and, by keeping costs low, have a low break-even point. For all of these reasons, flea markets constitute the largest segment of the $50 billion pop-up industry.

While some flea market vendors participate on a practically recreational basis, others make a handsome living from their involvement. So the first thing you should decide is whether you want this to be a source of incremental income, or whether you have the products and time to "go on the circuit" or take part in a long-term flea market and make a serious go of it as a flea market vendor.

You can usually hear about ongoing or upcoming flea markets by searching online and on local Craigslist announcements. Most flea markets are stand-alone destinations and are the only drawing card to attract customers. In an ideal world, you would be able to be a vendor at flea markets that also benefit from a customer base that happens to be there for other purposes as well. For example, PopUp Republic hosts a series of pop-up "handmade" outdoor markets on designated weekends at major malls across the country. On many such weekends, the malls draw upward of 50,000 shoppers—not visitors, mind you, but people who go there with money and the intention to buy things. We believe that these types of flea markets are the trendsetters for the modern flea market industry, especially since the malls have started to embrace them as attractions and income generators in themselves.

Although a flea market typically has a feel of a temporary bazaar, you still want your space to be as presentable and professional as possible. Having a tent or other enclosure, well-thought-out display tables, and attractive products are sensible and desirable.

If you sell clothing, it's a good idea to have a full-length mirror. In any case, you should be sure to come with lots of cash from which to make change; a credit card point-of-sale system, however rudimentary (most smartphones can be used with card readers that convert the phone into a credit card processor); bags; price tags; pens; business cards; and protective gear, insect-repellants, and aspirin.

While it is always difficult to ascertain ahead of time how much inventory to bring, here is one suggestion: Bring more than enough. This is good not only in order to maximize sales, but also because you always want your area to be "staged" right, and having a good supply of products will attract buyers.

When deciding what to sell at a flea market, you have a few choices. Of course, if you specialize in certain categories—if you make your own jewelry or clothing, for example—you will want to put all of your efforts toward marketing those items. But if you need to decide on what products to sell, then one of the most important elements for success is to source well and buy right. Find out who the most reputable flea market wholesalers are. Go to trade shows. Search the Internet. Become an expert in the types of products you intend to sell.

A study done by ProVendor in 2012 tallied up the top five selling categories at flea markets across the United States They were:

- Gifts and Novelties
- Fashion Accessories
- Apparel and Footwear
- Knives and Cutlery
- Sporting Goods

Tastes change, and surely new trends will bring about changes to what constitute bestsellers at flea markets. Of course, what to sell depends greatly on both the type of flea market it is and what the nearby demographics are, but do a little research and use a lot of common sense when deciding what to sell at flea markets. As with most commerce, the profits are generally made on the "buy side" rather than the "sell side."

One last thing: Simply because a flea market can be a one-off event with low entry fees and informal surroundings, that doesn't mean you should be a passive, low-key vendor. The principles of promoting and marketing yourself and your products still hold true. Make use of all the promotional avenues that are available to you: Craigslist; social media marketing; posters; community boards; they are all beneficial and should be put to maximum use in advance of and during the flea markets at which you are a vendor.

Yard Sales

B<small>ECAUSE</small> <small>POP-UPS</small> <small>ARE</small> considered to be a relatively recent phenomenon, it doesn't come naturally to think of yard sales as falling under the pop-up umbrella. After all, yard sales have been around for decades.

But by all definitions, yard sales are quintessential pop-ups. They tend to be one-off events, planned only weeks in advance, lasting but a few hours on a weekend, and without the benefit of the tools of the trade of advertising and marketing. And to be considered a pop-up, there has to be a physical presence of proprietors and participants. So a yard sale is certainly a pop-up.

One of the real advantages of a yard sale relates to their venues. The most traditional places at which to host yard sales are driveways and front stoops of personal residences and multi-family dwellings. No need to find a vacant storefront, and no expense associated with renting a booth at a fair or marketplace. Even logistical issues are reduced, such as how to take the merchandise that will be offered from where it is being kept, such as your attic or garage, to the end of the driveway. A good dolly can usually handle even the heaviest merchandise when it comes to bringing product to market. Despite some of the easier elements associated with executing effective yard sales, there are some very important steps you must undertake to make a yard sale a success.

The first thing to consider is that yard sales are more than informal home-based events—they are a national culture. Yard sale customers are avid, practically addicted. With the advent of mobile phone apps and GPS systems, many yard sale aficionados study upcoming yard sales, plan their routes, make sure to show up early for those that appear to have items that might be of most interest and benefit. They are not only believers, but are practically evangelical espousers of the proverb "one person's trash is another person's treasure."

One reason that yard sales personify pop-ups is that they are places where you can explore and find unique, one-of-a-kind items. FOMO—the fear of missing out—prevails at yard sales. This represents one of the biggest reasons why pop-up shops and pop-up restaurants have become so popular. There is the sense of discovery that people love to experience as part of their shopping journeys, and the fear that they may miss out on that long-lost Rembrandt that is being sold with an old $5 picture frame.

Our biggest advice to you if you are hosting a yard sale is to plan ahead. Some people think that if they are going to host a yard sale of items they basically just want to get rid of and make a little pocket change. They plan for it to take place on an otherwise unoccupied Sunday morning and think there is no need to do any planning—just get out there, bring a comfortable chair, bagel and cup of coffee, and just wing it. But that is far from the case. In fact, unless you plan to make some meaningful money and to sell the lion's share of what you are going to be offering, it may not be worthwhile to even hold a yard sale—you might be better off donating the items to charity for a tax write-off, or even just keeping them around for another ten years until you finally just throw them out. No matter how small, yard sales involve preparation—the successful yard sales involve a fair amount of work, and a lot of planning.

Okay, let's start with the obvious first steps. Pick a date, pick a time, and pick a place. Weekend mornings are the best. People have time to schedule and visit yard sales on weekends. Mornings are good because having it in the morning doesn't kill the whole day—not for you and not for the shopper. Second, you want to be on the shopper's scheduled routes and, if it is possible to be one of the first destinations rather than one of the last, your shoppers will have more money to spend at your sale. You might want to consider scheduling your yard sale to take place on a Saturday morning so that in case of inclement weather, you can pre-schedule a contingent rain date for the next morning, rather than waiting another week.

As for the location of your yard sale, unless you are participating in a public yard sale at a local school or church, you are likely planning to host your event at home. If possible, try to have your items displayed as close to the street as possible, since many prospects (including people who hadn't even known about your yard sale and just happen to be in the neighborhood) will slowly drive by, trying to determine whether your yard sale is one at which it is worthwhile to stop.

Next on the agenda is selecting the items you want to sell, arranging them, and pricing them appropriately. If you find an assortment of games that no one in the family ever plays any more and you are ready to sell them, make sure you have all of the pieces. If you are planning to sell clothing, be sure they are clean and display them either on hangers or neatly folded. In fact, make sure all of the items for sale are clean and, if possible, can be shown to be in good working order. People will be more inclined to buy used items and clothing if they feel they have been well kept. Start segregating your items by type in a designated "holding area." Put kitchen and household utensils in one area; books and games in another; sporting goods in a third; electronics in another; etc.

As for pricing, this can be tough, and there is no good rule of thumb to pass on. Keep in mind that clothes are rarely best-sellers at yard sales, so you might consider selling them at one uniform price and/or in multiple units (e.g., all clothing on this table $2 each, 3 for $5). Try to keep sentiment aside when trying to figure out how to price an item, especially clothing (if there is sentimental value involved, you might want to reconsider including it for sale in the first place). You basically have two top-down philosophies you can follow: You can figure out the maximum price you think you can command for an item and go that route, or you can figure out the lowest price you can sell an item for and still make it worth your while. Whatever you decide, put price tags on each item in a prominent place. You'll be thankful you did when customers are browsing through your collection.

One other notion to keep in mind when pricing is the means by which you will be paid. Let's start with cash, the most likely currency and the one you certainly prefer. Price in increments of $.25 those items you expect to sell for under $1.00. You want a bunch of quarters to be the only hard currency you have to carry. Many shoppers might only have dollar bills and it becomes cumbersome and time-consuming to have to make change for a 35-cent item (let alone a 71-cent item). Keep lots of singles and an adequate amount of five-dollar bills.

You might also want to be able to take credit card payments, especially if some of your items are a little pricey (say, $10 and up). These days, smartphones can be converted into credit card processors just by attaching a card reader to the phone, such as a Square. They are available at your local electronic stores for next to nothing (in some cases, actually nothing, as you will pay modest processing fees as you effect sales, which is how the manufacturer makes his money). Having credit card processing capability removes an issue for a buyer of not having carried enough cash with her to buy merchandise of interest.

Last, don't accept checks and don't give credit.

As you collect your items to sell, start thinking about how you can display them. On tables. In boxes. Hanging up. You may have to borrow some furniture and fixtures from neighbors. Start thinking about positioning. Keeping in mind that shopper who is slowly driving by, eyeballing what is for sale, you probably want to have some of your better items showcased closest to the street or where they are most easily seen.

You don't want to start marketing too soon. Yard sale shoppers are either serial yard sale shoppers and wait until they can look at the entire inventory of nearby yard sales before they plan their routes, or they are impromptu yard sale patrons who may not even plan their visit until the morning of the event. You want to post notices on all the local bulletin boards—at libraries, cafes, houses of worship, schools, etc. Although you will probably be tempted to post signs on telephone poles and mail boxes, make sure to check for local ordinances and their enforcement before you do this. If you have a green light, make the signs legible and be sure to remember to take them down when the event is over. (And while we are on the subject of local ordinances, take note of the fact that some towns require you to get prior approval for your yard sale and, in a few instances, there are fees associated with permission to host a yard sale).

In addition to the old-fashioned way of posting notices, take advantage of what social media marketing now enables you to do—for free. Posting a yard sale notice on Craigslist is a terrific way to expand your reach beyond your immediate neighborhood. Other local and hyperlocal media allow you to post notices for free as well, and you'd be wise to take advantage of this. Use your own Facebook circles and put the word out to your own network, and don't hesitate to ask "friends" to share with their friends, too.

On the day of the yard sale, be sure to be ready to go at the stated time. It's up to you whether you want to accommodate early birds. Many of those might be dealers, who like to get there before the big crowds in order to do some cherry picking. Again, it's your call. Everyone's cash is worth the same, and as long as someone is not trying to negotiate too low a price, you might be wise (and lucky) to have a dealer come by early to buy multiple items at the yard sale.

As you can see, yard sales do involve planning, good decision making, and some work. But I'm sure you will find that they can be a lot of fun, too, and you should meet some interesting, friendly shoppers during the course of the day.

The Ideal Pop-Up Customer

Why You Should Target Millennials

As with every business, the "target customer" can primarily be determined by three factors: your location, the products or services you are providing, and the demand for those products or services. For instance, one of our PopUp Republic clients is a Miami-based women's swimsuit designer who opened pop-up shops around the country (primarily in New York City) to promote her brand. This is a specific niche product that has a distinct target customer—females. Breaking it down one step further, in New York City, people only swim outdoors during the spring and summer months. So, unless the brand had a retail or pop-up presence in Miami, where it's based, or on the West Coast, where people swim outdoors year-round, the chances are that they were going to have to develop additional products or sell predominantly online to account for weather conditions and seasonality in their target markets.

Despite the customization needed to determine the targeted customers for the various types of pop-up concepts that exist, there is one very attractive group that is applicable to every type of brand across the board, no matter what's being sold or offered: Millennials. By definition, a Millennial is someone like me—born between 1980 and 2000 who is young (and naïve) enough to not know everything, but smart enough to significantly influence the way in which brands produce and promote their products and services.

We are seeing a significant rise in Millennial interaction with pop-ups. Given the popularity of social media within the last decade, these platforms are serving as an "instant feedback" tool for Generation Y, allowing them to instantly comment on news stories, sports scores or, perhaps more applicable, retail and dining trends and experiences.

Companies like Apple have contributed greatly as well. Since the first iPhone was launched in 2007, advancements such as texting, geo-location, and, of course, mobile applications (apps) have become the 21st century equivalents of letter writing, looking at maps and—dare I say it—reading books. Honestly, what did anyone do prior to cell phones? How did the world function?

Now, within a span of just a few years, uber no longer means "denoting an outstanding or supreme example of a particular kind of person or thing"; the terms "follow," "like," "pin it," and "check-in" are synonymous with the calls-to-action on many popular social networking sites; and every new startup is trying to be the "Air BnB of something." Plus, with the development of "tech" sites like VentureBeat, TechCrunch, Mashable, BuzzFeed, and many more, the reporting on buyouts, mergers, fundraises, new apps, and innovative technological phenomena is written about and dissected almost the instant they happen.

So what's my point? Millennials are the most avid users of social media, and as mentioned, pop-ups rely on social media to generate buzz and interest, and thus, your marketing efforts should reflect that.

When thinking about what I was going to write about in this chapter, I thought back to one of the coolest, most "Generation Y" pop-ups that I've ever heard about: in May 2014, a pop-up restaurant opened in London. This is not news, partly because my company was inspired by a trip to London, and according to The Telegraph (a popular U.K. media outlet), roughly 3.4 million pop-ups will open in London by 2017.

However, this pop-up was unique in that it mandated that its customers pay for their meals using Instagram.

Wait, what?

A popular frozen vegetable brand, Birds Eye, opened "The Picture House" pop-up restaurant in Manchester, U.K., as a means to promote both its brand and healthy frozen dining options. They fed hungry patrons and allowed them to pay for their meals via the popular social media site if they included the hashtag #BirdsEyeInspirations with their photos.

The fact that Birds Eye understood current consumer buying and interaction habits says a lot about how connected they are with their target market. They understand that the days of paying with cash are over, that there are apps that let you pay for your meal without actually taking any currency out of your pocket, and that people are using these apps, sites, and platforms in their everyday lives.

The biggest value that these social media platforms offer, though, is their social sharing features. As of the first quarter of 2015, there were 1.44 billion monthly active users on Facebook; 236 million active users on Twitter; and 300 million users on Instagram. For comparison's sake, the world population, as of June 2015, was 7.125 billion. If someone posts a picture of the dinner he is eating at the Birds Eye pop-up restaurant on Instagram, that image can, theoretically, spread to 299 million other people.

Social media platforms have suddenly become giant focus groups, capable of spreading messages, popular brands, user-generated content, live feedback, and apparently your dinner tonight, to millions of other individuals with the click of a single button.

So when someone asks you who the target demographic is for your next pop-up, your first answer should be "Millennials." They have the power to singlehandedly gravitate toward your brand and to make sure their friends, friends of friends, and followers of their friends of friends also know about your brand.

Case Study: The Launch of a Pop-Up Store

IN THE SUMMER of 2013, PopUp Republic approached the Brookline, Massachusetts, Economic Development Office with a proposal. It would oversee an effort to open and operate a pop-up shop marketplace in a particular district within an area of town called Brookline Village that historically had always been commercially challenged. Try as it might to energize that particular section of the neighborhood's local economy, the business community had never come up with the magic formula that would take hold there.

On the whole, Brookline Village's setting itself was quite charming, often bustling, and among long-time Brookline denizens, "The Village" had always had a particular allure. Its funky shops, eclectic and somewhat eccentric boutiques, and its ethnic restaurants had all given the neighborhood a unique personality that had been retained over the years. The Village also plays host to the iconic Puppet Showplace Theater, yoga studios, and holistic practitioners, and even a tucked-away television studio where PBS's much-adored *America's Test Kitchen* cooking show is produced. A very active subway line runs through The Village with a perfectly situated station right in the heart of the area, and abutting

Brookline Village is a major thoroughfare that provides a corridor between downtown Boston and the western suburbs.

But the area of The Village where PopUp Republic was suggesting that it would open up a pop-up shop did not draw pedestrian traffic from contiguous areas. It lacked sufficient parking and, as a consequence, the shops that did try to conduct business there rarely succeeded, making that major entryway into Brookline an uninviting portal to what was otherwise an upscale community. Maybe "uninviting" is too soft a portrayal—in reality, it was a blight, an embarrassment that town officials were hard-pressed to rectify.

Among the buildings that were located in that section of town was a multi-story mixed-use commercial/office building that was practically vacant despite being situated in a verdant, well-kept campus of buildings that were homes to largely medical and educational facilities. The building was owned by Boston Children's Hospital, which had well-publicized plans to completely raze and re-construct what was there. On the ground level of this building, called 2 Brookline Place, were six ground-level unoccupied storefronts, half of which served as storage rooms for the hospital's unused office furniture. The facilities management office of Children's Hospital was committed to being a good neighbor and had allowed various town-sponsored activities to take place in and around the building. But finding commercial tenants had been a problem, with word out that plans were afoot to tear down the building once regulatory approvals were received, and with the hospital hesitant to enter into long-term leases for those same reasons.

These made it a perfect venue for a pop-up. Many of the key ingredients were there:

- A vacant storefront with a motivated landlord was available on a short-term basis at a below-market rent (basically, the cost of the utilities).
- The local municipal economic development office was very much on board, as it had long been searching for ways to

energize commercial activity in that particular sector of town, with little success. Department heads agreed to work with PopUp Republic when it came to regulatory ordinances, introductions, and even promotion. It was a low-budget program that could reap benefits for the town and for nearby permanent merchants.

- Its location, while not prime, was adjacent to an active commercial area, an active subway stop, and a major thoroughfare. So if the pop-up could generate sufficient appeal and publicity, there were nearby shoppers from which to draw and ways to get there.

PopUp Republic negotiated a license to secure the storefront it had selected. Note: the relationship was governed by a license to use the property, not a lease. Many legal and financial obstacles were circumvented by entering into that sort of arrangement, something that prospective pop-up organizers and property managers should investigate before entering into a legal relationship with one another.

With a location in hand, plans were set in motion to launch the pop-up. Before the doors could open, the next step was to learn what ordinances affected the pop-up's launch and operation and what licenses had to be obtained and rules complied with.

There were more than a few. A license to conduct business was necessary to have in order to be compliant, even though this was a short-term enterprise. A temporary occupancy permit to conduct business within the site was also required. Certain considerations came to bear—the length of time of the temporary permit being sought proved to be important. Obtaining a permit for fewer than 30 days, followed by a sequence of 30-day renewals, helped ameliorate the stress that certain requirements would certainly have created—psychologically and financially—had a longer permit been sought and executed. The number of seats that would be used in the pop-up shop could lead to fire department restrictions not only in terms of maximum occupancy at any one time, but also as to whether a back room, which had a back door for an alternative egress point, could be used for storage or had to be kept clear. The size of signage, as related to the size of the front windows on which they would be hung, was stipulated by local ordinance. The signs themselves had to be approved. Access to public restrooms had to be provided.

Then there was the matter of food. For one thing, PopUp Republic was considering having food vendors participate, albeit with the product prepared offsite in a health department–approved facility. That opened up a new set of variables—permeability of the floor surface; availability of a hand-washing station; inspections by the health department; and so forth. In fact, it was determined that, even if food was not going to be sold at the pop-up market, the non-food vendors couldn't even serve coffee on site because of various provisions that precluded such activity from occurring. So food service was quickly eliminated from the overall scheme.

After that, insurance became the next issue to address (notice, we haven't even gotten to plans relating to what the pop-up itself was going to feature and sell!). The property manager had certain policy minimums and inclusions it wanted in the property insurance that were mandated. Of course, PopUp Republic wanted to be sure that an appropriate amount of property and casualty insurance was in place. Fortunately, this is a relatively easy task in most states and in most cases can be handled efficiently by a local insurance agent.

With location, licensing, and insurance in place, it was time to create the business plan for the pop-up itself. Which begs the question: Does one really need to put together a business plan for a one-off, temporary business? The answer is a resounding "yes." It doesn't have to be long, nor does it need to include sophisticated projections, but having a business plan as well as a budget goes a long way toward a successful outcome—even for a pop-up.

These issues are dealt with in greater detail in other chapters of this book, but consider it safe to say that PopUp Republic put in the effort to think about these issues and to plan for their implementation. The overall business strategy was clear: Enlist the participation of artisanal merchants, stay open from August through the Christmas holiday shopping season, then close by year's end. So it would be about a four-month pop-up, fairly long by pop-up shop standards, but still within a normal range.

Using social media and personal contacts, there was no shortage of candidates who were interested in participating, and a schedule was established as to who would be opening up shop when, and for how long. Each merchant was offered one of two options—either to run their business themselves (which made the most sense, as who better to sell their merchandise than those who made the items?), for which there was one financial arrangement, or to have PopUp Republic's staff handle their business, in which case another financial arrangement was offered.

A reporting and transactional system was established for both. In the case in which PopUp Republic's staff had the duties to sell product on behalf of the merchants, a point-of-sale system was needed that would accommodate the business envisioned. We chose one that was very economical and efficient and could be transacted through anyone's smartphone.

Incidentally, finding temporary staffing is not something that should be downplayed or left to the last minute. There is a sizable pool of experienced retail people available for part-time, temporary work, but tapping that pool and arranging a schedule requires planning and flexibility on both sides.

While the Brookline Village pop-up had some extra steps required by virtue of having to coordinate schedules among both the vendors and its staff, it had the offsetting benefit of not having to worry about inventory. This is an issue that should be well-thought-out in advance: how much to produce, how much to bring to the pop-up for sale, and other distribution options for liquidation of inventory not sold at the pop-up.

With the venue, licensing, insurance, staffing, and transaction costs now in place, PopUp Republic was able to turn its attention to such matters as signage and supplies that would be needed on a daily basis. It was then able to determine its break-even and to concentrate the majority of its remaining time and resources to promoting and marketing the merchants and the pop-up itself. It reached out to local television media and, sure enough, sparked enough interest so that a local network affiliate sent a reporter and cameraman to broadcast a very nice story about the pop-up. This not only trans-lated into an increase in pedestrian traffic, who were curious to find out what this "pop-up thing" was all about, but cast a positive light on the local economic development department and its efforts to support the local business community (PopUp Republic made sure to invite local economic development officials to be there and be interviewed when the cameras were rolling). Additional outreach to other local media, supplemented by a consistent social media mar-keting campaign, and even the old-fashioned marketing method of posting notices on nearby public bulletin boards and keeping it up during the duration of the pop-up, all went far in promoting the Brookline Village Pop-Up Marketplace and led to a successful four-month run at what was previously an empty commercial wasteland.

In summary, upon deciding to open up a pop-up shop, decide on an area where you would like to establish the business. Secure a location, seeking the help of local town officials and the local business community. Arrange for obtaining all required licenses and permits (make friends with the officials in charge!) and for adequate insurance coverage. Determine the number of staff you will need and line them up early in the process. Go to your local office supply store and purchase a point-of-sale system; inventory control software (if relevant); and various supplies (don't forget trash bags and trash receptacles); hang out your shingle; promote your pop-up store; and enjoy the excitement of going into business on your own!

Pop-Up Checklist

Phase 1: The Set-Up

☐ Find a location. Options can include empty storefronts, existing stores, existing restaurants, your driveway, an individual's home, the local park, and many others. Be creative!

☐ Secure all permits and licenses. Visit your local town hall to find out what is required.

☐ Ask your landlord about requirements: rent, hours of operation, maintenance staff, parking, equipment/furniture usage, etc.

☐ Buy insurance: general liability, Workers' Compensation, and other insurance may be required by your landlord.

☐ Lay out your pop-up. Visit your pop-up space and figure out its configuration and aesthetic design. (How will you display your products? Where will your tables and chairs go?)

☐ Purchase equipment, fixtures, furniture, supplies, point-of-sale systems, and anything else you would need to outfit your space and manage your pop-up.

☐ Create window displays, signs, and banners. Have everything printed at a local print shop.

☐ Hire your staff.

☐ Determine your goal. Do you want to build your brand? Simply test out your products? See what it's like to have a retail presence? This will help as you operate your pop-up.

Phase 2: The Operation

☐ Determine your pop-up's policies (Are pets allowed? Public restrooms?)
☐ Set your hours of operation.
☐ Promote your pop-up!
☐ Do something to draw people in. You can promote it all you want online, but how about those who walk by? Balloons, live music, and lemonade stands are a few creative ways to draw attention to your pop-up.
☐ Determine the policies for your staff. Make sure they are approachable, knowledgeable, and successfully represent your brand!
☐ Get some swag, whether it's t-shirts, pens, stickers, or mugs, there are cost-effective promotional tools you can use to help build your brand!
☐ Organize events! If you are planning a long-term pop-up, why not organize events, parties, or get-togethers with the community?
☐ Maintain contact with your landlord. Whether you're open for two hours or two months, a happy landlord is important.

Phase 3: The Evaluation

☐ Clean up the space.
☐ Disassemble all displays, furniture, banners and signs, and any furniture you customized for your pop-up.
☐ Ask yourself: Would I do it again? Did I accomplish my goal(s)?
☐ Determine net profits.
☐ Thank your landlord!

What's Ahead

THE POP-UP INDUSTRY has made tremendous strides lately, particularly over the last three years as it has evolved here in the United States. No longer are pop-ups just traditional brick-and-mortar businesses, but instead, as we have discussed in this book, they are pop-up shops, pop-up restaurants, supper clubs, food and fashion trucks, farmers markets, flea markets, and lemonade stands that open in all sorts of locations.

Despite being temporary in nature, it is clear that pop-ups are here to stay. This section will forecast the future, discuss what's popular in the industry now, and predict where things can expect to go in the next three years and beyond.

Reload, Fire, Aim

WHETHER OR NOT its concepts are still considered as sacrosanct as they originally were, *In Search of Excellence* continues to be one of the best-selling business management books in the world. Written by Tom Peters and Robert Waterman and published in 1982 by HarperCollins, it has been dubbed "The Best Business Book of All Time" by reviewers and academics. The book identifies eight themes that are the common elements among 43 companies that Peters and Waterman studied, evaluated, and deemed "excellent."

The theme that has been cited—and followed—most often through the years is represented by the title of one of the book's chapters: Ready, Fire, Aim. The lesson taught is that the great companies have a bias toward action and don't waste a lot of time discussing what *might* work. They keep management meetings to a minimum and are comfortable using a methodology in which they make mistakes and learn from those mistakes, rather than trying to figure it all out in advance.

We don't know whether Mark Zuckerberg, the co-founder of Facebook, ever read *In Search of Excellence* (for one thing, the book is still required reading in many colleges, and Zuckerberg dropped out of Harvard in his sophomore year), but the two mantras associated with Facebook sure sound like variations on the theme: "Done is better than perfect" and "Move Fast and Break Things."

Both slogans make the assertion that being prone toward getting things done, even if they aren't fully ready, is better than obsessing about every last detail. A business plan is never going to be totally complete and accurately predictive. At some point, you have to pull the trigger. Peters, Waterman, and Zuckerberg feel the shooting should begin fairly early in the process.

Generally speaking, this theory of how to run a business is often pivotal in leading a business toward its ultimate right path. All of the great business plans, all of the projections and modeling and prototyping, will often quickly fall by the wayside as soon as a plan starts to be implemented. It is incredible how many well-known companies started off doing one thing, but very quickly adapted to new realities and turned into something entirely different as they began executing their business.

A perfect example of this is Groupon, one of the fastest growing companies of all time. Started in 2007 by Anthony Mason under its original name, The Point, the company quickly embarked on a fast pace toward oblivion. As it started a wind-down process, making preparations to return money to its investors, it realized that its central tenet, tipping-point-based collective action, could apply to local business advertising. So it made a now famous pivot and re-launched in November 2008 as Groupon, and within 16 months reached a $1 billion valuation.

The philosophy of "Ready, Fire, Aim" does have its detractors, however, and many examples of companies that went to market too soon with products or services that were not ready for public consumption are just as legendary as Groupon and Facebook. Going to market prematurely, with a full financial and staffing commitment and a total focus toward one singular objective, can be disastrous for a business if its vision turns out to be myopic. It can be the death knell of what otherwise would have been a fabulous idea and a lucrative business.

The conclusion is that proclivity toward action, even if not fully ready for prime time, can be the key to success . . .or it can be catastrophic. So what can one do to increase the pace of acceleration by leaping before you look, while at the same time mitigating the risk of doing so?

This is another way in which pop-ups present themselves as a better alternative. For an artisan, chef, or brand that wants to launch a new product or service or open up a new market, pop-ups can serve as the equivalent of beta tests, incorporating an interactive process through the organizing of serial pop-ups. Pop-ups are not just ends in themselves. They can also be tactics used to effect strategies and trial runs. Do it over and over until it is perfected. And *then*, launch it as a full-fledged permanent business, with the risk drastically reduced. Load, and then keep re-loading, firing away, tweaking and experimenting, aiming until you are closer and closer to the target.

What worked for Anthony Mason and Mark Zuckerberg might not work for everyone. It took tactical brilliance, business acumen, and a fair amount of good fortune. Often, the television character that most exemplifies a start-up entrepreneur is the inimitable Mr. Magoo. He keeps moving forward, completely unaware of the bombs and boulders falling all around him.

A start-up by its nature can (and usually is) chaotic, as it is almost impossible to institute systems *before* execution of the plan actually begins. Rather, the process is more like "Execute—Systematize—Execute some more—Systematize some more—Revamp and pivot—Systematize some more," and so on. More than walking a straight line, it's like a complicated dance step, but with no pre-established choreography.

It is clear how pop-ups can help immeasurably in terms of saving money and time. Instead of moving a huge operation in one direction, only to have to retrace one's steps and do it again and again, pop-ups are a means by which to have trial runs, to see what works and what doesn't, try it again, and then, when it's time to start the "real deal," be able to have some systems in place that make sense and rationalize the entire operation from the get-go.

Running serial pop-ups also can help develop brand awareness before a permanent business is officially launched. The professional culinary field in particular is renowned for how tough it is to break into. Traditionally, the hierarchy to mount and dues to be paid are legendary—you plan to be a dish washer, a server, line staff, maybe rising to sous chef, then a chef working for someone else, until maybe, just maybe, you find the way to open a restaurant of your own.

This is true throughout the industry and across the country. But imagine what it is like in established capitals of cuisine, such as New York City, Chicago, Los Angeles, and other cities, where there are restaurants in the thousands, some headed by celebrity chefs, including those that have been there for decades. The idea of establishing a new restaurant in such settings is more than merely daunting—it can be mission impossible!

With the recent growth of the pop-up restaurant and food truck industries, however, there is now a new path toward the goal of opening a restaurant. Slowly but surely, step by step, aspiring chefs—even those with no formal culinary training—have a new way to establish their identities and to build a following. In fact, those who have opted for careers in public dining can go the traditional route *and also* operate periodic pop-ups side by side—making a living while building the foundation of a future restaurant.

But that's pop-up restaurants. How about other types of pop-ups, such as pop-up shops? They deal with a whole host of other variables and challenges. For every aspiring chef, there are hundreds of aspiring artisans, designers, and collectors, all of whom are in the retail business—or wanting to start.

It might be true that *anyone* can open a pop-up shop, but not everyone can open a pop-up restaurant; however, that doesn't mean it is easier to do the former. On the contrary, at least in terms of quantity, the number of obstacles that have to be overcome is greater when it comes to pop-up retail than when it applies to pop-up dining. So how do fledgling entrepreneurs get into the retail business, especially if their hope is to have their own brand? Again, there is a traditional route one follows to ascend to the higher echelons of the retail industry. You work the sales counter, you work behind the scenes, but there are many levels to climb and skills to master, and there is always someone competing for your job. However strong and recognized a company might be, there isn't much security in the retail business. In one of author Joseph Heller's great books, *Something Happened*, the picture is painted very clearly—there is always going to be someone at a level just above you who is afraid you are going to go after his job, and there is always going to be someone just below you who is going to be after yours. Insecurity reigns at every level, and that is the world of retail as we know it. Historically, that has been the only avenue available to climb the heights of retail.

Except now, when pop-ups provide another route to take. A better, smarter route, one that gives you the opportunity to exhibit your talents and sell your goods or services, but in a fun, orderly way. Even if, at the outset, you have to hold down a steady job as you launch your alternative professional pursuits, pop-ups enable you to start your business and to follow your dreams.

An essential element of launching a successful pop-up shop is to differentiate yourself from the pack, especially from the products and services that are offered everywhere—in big stores, malls, online, outlets, wherever. Remember why consumers go to pop-ups: They want a shopping *experience*. They want to know who made the product or whose tastes led to the collection of goods before them. They want to know where the product was made, and how. They'd like to learn the "story" behind the product they are considering buying.

And most of all, pop-up shop consumers want to do more than just consume. They want to curate. They want to manifest their own tastes by finding things that are different, that are *exclusive*. Shopping is a creative outlet, or at least it should be. That is one reason why pop-up shops are so popular. With so many chains and the sterile online stores offering the same or similar items, that exclusivity is gone, the ability to express oneself is gone, the knowledge of who made the product, how it was made, and where it was made are virtually impossible to discover. Pop-up shops are the inverse of big brand, online commerce—and although it sounds somewhat oxymoronic, the more retail is co-opted by the big brands and e-commerce, the more opportunity there will be for pop-up entrepreneurs to gain a foothold among discerning shoppers.

In looking at the future of the pop-up industry, we can identify features that have catapulted them from merely being trendy to being trendsetting mainstays. They provide many features and opportunities that conventional commerce cannot and never will. They are an outgrowth of many converging movements—the sharing economy, D-I-Y, Shop Local, even online commerce with its impersonal way of doing business. Pop-ups might be short-lived, but as an industry we foresee a very long shelf life.

Interview with Shuchi Naidoo, Founder of Twenty-Nine Calories Pop-Up Restaurant

SHUCHI NAIDOO IS the founder of Twenty Nine Calories, an innovative pop-up dining concept that creates modern Indian-inspired tasting menus for supper clubs, pop-up dinners, and private dining experiences in New York City. She has also partnered with large brands, such as West Elm, to create an enhanced, one-of-a-kind experience for customers.

Q: What is your culinary background?

None. I am a self-taught chef. I have always enjoyed cooking and am constantly practicing, experimenting, researching, and observing to hone my skills.

Q: What led you to using pop-ups as one of the ways you promote and conduct business?

They're fun, unique, and non-monotonous. The foundation of my business is to be creative, and pop-ups allow just that. With

(continued)

(continued)
out-of-the-ordinary spaces, decor, ideas, themes, and partnerships to work with, the sky is the limit when it comes to differentiating yourself.

Q: How many pop-up restaurants have you hosted, and when did you begin? How hard is it to organize and operate a pop-up? Do you think that the more you've done, the more successful they've been? Do you enjoy hosting them?

Oh my, I doubt I have a count, but I would say at least ten since I started in June 2014 (so less than a year!). I'd say it's pretty tricky to organize a pop-up restaurant. Having a new space to work with every time requires checklists, careful planning, organization, and buckets of patience! Not to mention energy, since I am a one-man team. But it's also that much more rewarding when you see it to completion. Every event is a learning experience, and each better than the last. My following has greatly increased since my first one in June 2014 (when I was struggling to sell ten tickets) to a sell-out in just 24 hours now for events up to 20 guests. I must be doing something right.

I love hosting pop-ups. Food is my means to share my story, meet and connect with inspiring individuals, and create memorable experiences.

Q: What is your ultimate goal?

To become the best at what I do. The great thing about the combination of food and a pop-up is that neither confines you to an idea or style. I want to keep evolving, grow with feedback, create larger partnerships, and one day be the go-to person for unique dining experiences, all while showcasing a new side of Indian cuisine.

Q: Tell me a little about yourself. What inspired you to cook?

I started cooking when I could barely reach the kitchen counter. Born and raised in northern India, I spent the majority of my childhood in a boarding school. With insipid cooking and heartless meals, I craved the holidays that were spent watching mum cook for her "home-food-starved" children. It was as though she stuffed all her love into those delectable bites and, yet, never ran out of it. I used to love how she played with simple Indian ingredients and indulged in an ever-so-stylish presentation. She made it look like art. And today, with no formal culinary training, it is that very enthusiasm that defines my passion. Investment banker turned private chef, I started this business to design meals that are about much more than individuals cooking food. I wanted to host experiences that would be an adventure.

29. Private Kitchen is a social dining concept creating prix-fixe tasting menus for supper clubs, pop-up dining experiences, and private events. Centered around small plates and tapas inspired by the unexposed genre of home-style Indian cuisine, I am giving "curry" a pretty significant facelift. I use creative food as a medium to connect, inspire, and collaborate with individuals and businesses alike, and my floating kitchen allows me to develop that magic every day! Menus are secret till the day, inspired by native roots and the ever-changing seasons.

Chef Shuchi Naidoo Prepares for Her Pop-Up Dinner.

Look Out! Here Come the Big Brands and the Big Malls

When thinking about pop-ups, what quickly comes to mind is the word "aspiring." Aspiring chefs, aspiring designers, aspiring artisans. When it comes to pop-up spaces, the first thought one usually has is an empty storefront, possibly located on a main street that is well past its heyday and trying to bootstrap its return to relevance. In truth, both characterizations are still very common-place in the universe of pop-ups.

But right before our eyes, the pop-up world is undergoing a sea change. Over the past several years, well-known brands have become very involved in the pop-up movement. Nike, Kate Spade, Louis Vuitton, Target, West Elm, and hundreds more have been participants in the phenomenon. They've been joined by celebrity pop-ups, such as Kanye West, the Kardashians, One Direction, and even NFL and Major League sports teams. Well-known chefs such as Daniel Boulud, Marcus Samuelsson, and other culinary superstars have joined the parade. Leading shopping mall owner/operators such as Simon Malls, General Growth Properties, Westfield, and Federal Realty are all jockeying for position to be participants. Perhaps most surprising of all, many of the online-only retailers who have eschewed the notion of operating physical stores have recognized that consumers are demanding more than just convenience when choosing where to shop.

What's going on?

Many factors are creating the conditions by which the pop-up market is changing. For one thing, something connotes "fresh" and "exclusive" just by invoking the word "pop-up" or talking about pop-up destinations. Think about your visceral reaction to these two exclamations:

"I'm going shopping at the supermarket!"

"I'm going shopping at the farmers market!"

The first one invokes a "so what" type of reaction at best. In fact, it is probably an activity that is one of the regular chores that appear on a typical weekly to-do list. But while a visit to the local farmers market might also be a weekly event, a not-uncommon response might very well be "May I go, too?"

Farmers markets, particularly those that are open seasonally or have different merchants at different times of the year, are quintessential pop-ups. They reflect the consumer penchant for a "shop local" and "discover something new" shopping experience. This kind of natural reaction is what national retailers—be they offline or online—and shopping malls want to capture. They want that "guilt by association," but in the case of pop-ups, it is "benefit by association."

The participation by national brands also reflects a recognition that perhaps the pendulum has swung too far toward online retailing, leaving consumers thirsty for what has always been a major component of satisfied customers—the personal attention and shopping experience that is only offered by a local, physical presence. The message shoppers are sending is that virtual reality is great, but reality is even better.

Complementing this evolution is the role played by the major malls. The big malls have been running scared. They have witnessed the significant and growing encroachment by online retail. They have seen population migrations that ended up differing from what their prognostications had led them to believe. They have felt firsthand the new consumer devotion to local producers and small businesses.

The first response by the malls and big box stores was to close many of their underperforming properties as quickly as possible. They saw it as a lost cause in many cases and wanted to cut their losses. They also looked at what the online retailers were doing to attract customers and tried to copy them. For example, we know of one of the largest mall operators in the country that invested in a next-day delivery start-up in the hopes of replicating the shipping advantages being offered by e-commerce businesses. The reaction by the malls and the big box stores was reactive and defensive, rather than trying to figure out creative ways in which they might fit into the new equation.

But then something started to change, led by both consumer sentiment and sheer economics. Shoppers began to frequent physical manifestations of stores—not just new spiffy settings, but even (maybe especially!) throwbacks to the old ways in which merchandise was bought and sold—directly from the maker, or if not from the original producer, at least from someone to whom they could talk about the product. Flea markets, farmers markets, seasonal marketplaces, and yes, pop-up stores began to spring up everywhere, from the trendsetting cities such as New York and Los Angeles to small towns and neighborhoods across the country.

This gave the major brands and the big malls a reason to pause and reflect. The big brands, particularly the online retailers, had sworn off the big financial and time commitments associated with running permanent physical stores. Offline commerce was totally at odds with the more streamlined ways they wanted to run their businesses. Malls, needing to generate cash flow from leases in order to service debt and fund operations, had always considered long-term five-and-ten-year leases, even longer, as the only sustainable model.

But perhaps the new times were showing them a new path forward! Perhaps temporary tenancies were the way to bridge the gap. Maybe the online retailers could learn some lessons from their offline retail counterparts, and perhaps the malls had to recognize that the big brands were ready to showcase their goods in physical locations, but not on a long-term basis. This gave rise to a new term—omnichannel—a relatively seamless way in which retailers could market their goods across many channels—online, offline, on television, through the written media—and do it in all the major markets, but without having to commit to major buildouts and permanent staffing.

The obvious solution was pop-ups. Suddenly, pop-ups became cutting-edge, a way for big brands and big malls to lend their sophistication, expertise, and most importantly, their existing infrastructures and market dominance, to the nascent pop-up movement. They weren't *replacing* the artisanal sector from the pop-up world; they were expanding the very usage of pop-ups in unexpected ways.

Online commercial stalwarts such as Amazon, Microsoft, Google, and many others launched new products or featured certain items or services by going the pop-up route. So did many national brands. But because these larger, established companies favored the advantages offered by shopping centers, they opted for the malls for their physical set-ups, rather than individual storefronts. The malls eagerly accommodated them, establishing special programs and even spaces that are dedicated to peripatetic merchants rather than stationary ones. It was a new day, and the big brands and the big malls wanted in.

The malls also recognized another opportunity that was being afforded by the emerging pop-up industry. The malls had a unique issue. You can even call it a problem. By their very nature, malls tended to have large common areas that set the stage for the individual storefronts, and because most malls were commuter-based, they needed huge parking lots. As a result, a majority of the space that made up the mall entity was underutilized, at least as far as revenue generation was concerned.

Almost as if a light bulb went off for all of them, pop-ups appeared on the horizon as a way to create new pockets of incremental income. The intent wasn't just to attract increased foot traffic to the malls on behalf of their tenants. No, the malls wanted to make money themselves from the pop-ups that would be run on their properties.

In one of our early meetings with representatives of one of the major mall operators in the United States, this message was made loud and clear. Our discussions centered on a variety of pop-ups we could help organize and curate—farmers markets, food truck festivals, pop-up restaurants, holiday-season marketplaces, food crawls, and more—and all had to include one integral component: the malls had to make money from them. They weren't inclined to become only entertainment destinations. Their objective was primarily "Show me the money!"

This made so much sense. One of the opportunities we recognized from the outset of our own business development was that there were many venues that were not being optimally used, that were actually closed more hours than they were open (!), and that could easily and profoundly benefit by incorporating pop-up events and spaces into their planning.

As this book is being written, our expectation is that any sequel in the future would include the geometric increases in the uses of pop-up enterprises at common areas such as those within malls and at parking lots and other public spaces that are currently underutilized and underperforming.

Interview with Melinda Holland, SVP of Business Development, General Growth Properties

GENERAL GROWTH PROPERTIES (GGP) is the second-largest shopping mall owner/operator in the United States, with over 120 U.S.-based properties in their portfolio. They have also become leaders among their peers for the pop-up concepts they organize at many of their shopping centers nationwide, using these experiences as opportunities for enhanced foot traffic and additional revenue opportunities.

Melinda Holland and Patty Hirt, two GGP employees at the forefront of the company's efforts to incorporate pop-ups into their business strategy, were kind enough to answer a few questions.

Q: Why would you say malls are better than empty storefronts, urban centers, and stand-alone locations to host a pop-up?

Malls not only provide built-in traffic, but an opportunity to provide unique experiences for guests. In-mall pop-up stores attract
(continued)

(*continued*)

a diverse shopper mix, including families, Millennials, and Baby Boomers. In addition, malls support emerging brands with additional P.R., research, marketing, technology, and partnership services that aren't necessarily guaranteed in a stand-alone space. GGP also owns urban properties, so we have a unique understanding of what these storefronts can provide.

Q: How did GGP become a leader in turning malls into popular pop-up venues?

At GGP we strive to create an exceptional experience for our shoppers; therefore we have to be progressive in our thinking regarding current and future retailers. We've seen a fascinating trend of customers wanting unique, handcrafted products and merchandise. Accordingly, GGP became an early adopter in disrupting the mall experience by launching pop-up shops with dynamic brands, experiential activations (such as DreamWorks Adventure to Santa), and establishing a food and drink division, focusing solely on unique dining, group and social gatherings at our malls.

Q: Given the many properties in GGP's portfolio, it seems to be the perfect fit for brands of all sizes who want to expand their growth. Can you provide a glimpse into the process by which a brand can open its pop-up with GGP?

GGP is always looking for new, emerging brands. We work with companies doing new brand launches and experiential activations. We have a pop-up specialist at each mall as well as a national retail development team. If you are interested in opening in a nearby mall, call the mall office to set up a meeting with a specialist. During this meeting, we learn about the brand's objectives for popping-up, target audience, and budget. Our specialist can than assess costs based on space, location, and marketing needs as well as any permits or licenses you might need to open. We've seen brands go from pop-up to permanent and from small brands to big brands. It also is not uncommon to meet with a retailer on Wednesday and have them open for business on Saturday.

In the real estate business, the most important thing is location. Our corporate team makes it easy to launch a pop-up in top DMAs so brands can focus on storytelling, customer experience, and bringing the brand to life.

Interview with Patty Hirt, Retail Development at General Growth Properties

GENERAL GROWTH PROPERTIES (GGP) is the second-largest shopping mall owner/operator in the United States, with over 120 U.S.-based properties in their portfolio. They have also become leaders among their peers for the pop-up concepts they organize at many of their shopping centers nationwide, using these experiences as opportunities for enhanced foot traffic and additional revenue opportunities.

Melinda Holland and Patty Hirt, two GGP employees at the forefront of the company's efforts to incorporate pop-ups into their business strategy, were kind enough to answer a few questions.

Q: Online retail is probably going to garner 10 percent of the total market this year. How are malls reacting to this new form of competition? How are malls changing?

GGP is a future-ready organization. In order to deliver the experiences consumers are demanding, we have to be nimble. We still

(continued)

(continued)

exercise tried-and-true best practices, but we also embrace change and omnichannel retailing. We don't see online shopping as a threat—we see it as a complement to the physical store. Pop-ups represent that change; many are pure play online retailers looking to experiment, garner real-time and real-life feedback. Pop-ups also increase repeat visits to the mall. In this digital age we look at our malls as websites and keep the content fresh, relatable, and cutting-edge.

Q: We at PopUp Republic used to have a hard time getting malls to entertain having pop-ups temporarily fill empty storefronts. Now, the opposite is true. What happened?

I have been in the mall industry for more than 20 years specializing in pop-up, and it has certainly evolved. Our experience in working side by side with local indie retailers to develop their brand in a brick-and-mortar setting has led us to understand the inherent challenges these entrepreneurs face. This insight has allowed us to create a winning formula for everyone involved. With this, brands recognize the value of pop-ups and creating an offline experience and correlate GGP with success due to our innovation and business approach, locations with built-in traffic, and a developed social media base.

Q: We are also seeing malls make use of underutilized assets—namely, parking lots and common areas—to generate incremental income. You are at the vanguard of this trend. What kinds of pop-ups do you see fulfilling this vision and filling these areas?

We are seeing pop-up markets and flash sales under tents in our parking lots. I've been approached by everything from a pop-up movie theater complete with concessions to a large-scale horse theater. In the world of food trucks, most cities have predetermined locations for these businesses, which is great, but logistical *challenges can be detrimental to business. GGP has seen success with pop-up food truck markets at our malls.*

As for the common areas, we will see brands interested in engaging in a sensory experience with consumers. The moment consumers enter the mall, the ambiance, aromas from the coffee shops, and tactile experiences from touching the merchandise enhance the shopper experience. Colors, designs, vignettes, and displays provide consumers with visual stimulation, which is what pop-ups deliver at their best.

Pop-Ups

Why They Are Becoming Permanent

OUR CRYSTAL BALL was fairly opaque just a few years ago when it came to prognosticating the future of the pop-up industry. We were in the midst of a maelstrom—the Internet was exploding, new software was coming out daily, smartphones were becoming the new computer of choice. Big stores were shrinking, big malls were expanding. New buzzwords and phrases such as "social media marketing" and "omnichannel" were upending business models as if there were no tomorrow—and for some business models, it would become clear that, in fact, there was going to be no tomorrow. Adapt, adapt quickly, or you'll be gone. Blockbuster, Radio Shack, you'd best be looking over your shoulder.

As retailers and food purveyors were trying to assess what was going on all around them and reacting on the fly to new circumstances they were totally ill-prepared to encounter, there was a reversion to what had worked best in the past, but with accommodations for the new facts on the ground. Our abilities to foresee the future of pop-ups were helped when we started to define what, in fact, constituted a pop-up.

Pop-ups are identifiable mostly by their temporary natures. It might be for a few moments, it might be seasonal, it might even be for a longer period, but pop-up shops, pop-up restaurants, and pop-up events became known for their one-off characteristics. They came, they conquered, and they went. There was no need for big buildouts. There was no mandate to have long-term commitments. No full-time staffs were required.

Technological advances helped a lot. Being able to have WiFi anywhere one wanted to pitch a tent connected merchants to their headquarters, even if headquarters was located largely within the very portable phone they were holding. Having mobile, onsite P.O.S. devices enabled merchants to be paid via credit cards, which by now are the most common currency used by shoppers, and will enable pop-ups to be paid in the future if payments-by-phone become the new method of choice for concluding transactions.

Another common feature of pop-ups is their personal nature, something that shoppers still crave, notwithstanding their love of convenience. Shoppers love to find out the story behind what they buy and what they eat. Where was it made? How was it grown? Who made it? How does it look on me? Is this something everybody else has, or can I have it exclusively?

Shopping is part buying, part exploring. Think about it. Going from parlor to parlor, booth to booth during an open artist studio event (one of our favorite types of pop-up) is as much about impromptu discovering as it is about buying a piece of art. Open artist studios offer the rare opportunity to find new works of art and talk to emerging, immensely talented artists. Rarely do they open their studios to the public—it happens only once or twice a year, maybe just for a day or two. And then the doors shut. The FOMO factor rears its head, and going to open artist studios is not just a shopping escapade, it is something you put on the calendar, not to be missed.

When put that way, one can more easily identify what a pop-up is. A booth at a flea market that offers handmade accessories guarantees a certain level of craftsmanship, especially if it is a product of the merchant himself. Although we are confronted by produce every time we enter a supermarket, there is something special about meandering through the stalls of local farmers at a farmers market, finding heads of cabbage that are twice as big as the local grocery store's, knowing also that it was grown by a local farmer just a few miles down the road.

Pop-up retail stores are becoming prevalent now that the big malls are opening their vacant storefronts to pop-up merchants. Malls are always finding a need to remain fresh and relevant, and what better way than to host unexpected and unique pop-up shops within their confines? Pop-up shops not only provide new artisanal stores to attract shoppers, but also create incremental rental income opportunities between permanent residencies.

Other types of pop-ups are also springing up at the major malls, as mall operators have realized their malls can become entertainment destinations and that their common areas, including their parking lots, can become venues for one-off shopping events. Farmers markets are now becoming popular events in mall parking lots, as are food truck festivals. Roaming art galleries, local artisanal fairs, family festivals, and many other temporary commercial happenings are now being regularly scheduled in all sorts of venues.

Pop-up dining has found a home on the public cuisine scene as well. The Taste of Chicago, the world's largest food festival held in one place at one time, is now highlighted by its roster of pop-up restaurants. Restaurant Day is an international festival of pop-up restaurants hosted by thousands of individuals, often at individual households, held four times a year all over the world. Diner en Blanc is a clandestine outdoor picnic that takes place at unannounced public venues in scores of international cities. Secret supper clubs take place at all times and places—there is probably one that goes on in your neighborhood without you even being aware of it.

Of course, there are the now-unstoppable food trucks. They are a force that local regulators are now having to deal with. They are cheap, and they are good. Street food is as much a part of the local culture as the neighborhoods in which they appear, and food carts and trucks are a new way in which entrepreneurialism is being encouraged and fostered.

So while some pop-ups might seem dated—vegetable vendors used to walk the streets selling their produce, farmers have always sold their food from farm stands—they are far more than throwbacks to nostalgic times. Pop-ups are ways in which commerce is adapting to new technologies and new customer preferences. If that includes a weird confluence of omnichannel, online marketing, mobile phones, farm stands, food trucks, small artist studios, and million-square-foot malls, then so be it. The future is about cherry-picking the best of what each age and sector has to offer and, in many ways, the future is manifesting itself in the form of pop-ups. Temporary, but here to stay.

Why Pop-Ups Make Sense for Baby Boomers

WHEN IT COMES to Baby Boomers and pop-ups, there's good news and there's bad news. The good news is that they are living longer, as life expectancies keep moving up. With this longevity has come better healthcare, better medicines, and better understanding of what a healthy lifestyle entails. As a consequence, people are not only living longer, but they are also living better.

The bad news is that Baby Boomers are living longer, with a prolonged need for subsistence and for the resources to support an active way of life. Unfortunately, most Boomers have not made enough money nor socked away enough savings to accommodate their needs, with such national support services as Social Security and Medicare unable to provide enough financial assistance to cover the needs of the senior population after they retire. Simply put, they are leaving their jobs and careers not having made enough money to satisfy their financial needs for the remainder of their lives.

Alongside that dilemma is the fact that many Boomers are not ready to simply retire and stop all productive activities. In fact, in many cases, the opposite is true. They don't consider themselves to be "playing the back nine." Rather, they feel they are "playing

36 holes." Having worked all of their adult lives at jobs that perhaps did not fulfill their ambitions and dreams, they are looking at retirement as being their golden age, when they are finally free to go after pursuits that they had deferred while having to earn a living at jobs that did not match their personal and professional goals.

There are currently approximately 75 million Baby Boomers (ages 51 to 69) in the United States. The vast majority of them retain their cognitive and physical abilities and are looking at their post-retirement years as being more than just a well-deserved time to slow down. They are entering a new stage, with options and opportunities not all that different from those that are presented to Millennials. They have a second chance to decide what meaningful things they can do with their lives.

There are virtually the same number of Millennials today as there are Boomers. One trend in which the two groups are moving in opposite directions relates to the country's workforce. More than one-third of American workers today are Millennials (ages 18 to 34). This share of the labor force is increasing and has now surpassed that of the Baby Boomers, who continue to retire from the labor force.

The Baby Boomers are perhaps in the best position to start businesses, especially with all of the possibilities that the pop-up movement provides. Millennials are starting their careers, laying foundations for their climb up the professional ladder. Millennials are starting families. Millennials are accumulating assets and, with that, they are accumulating debt. They are not in a great position, whether in terms of finances or their new responsibilities, to launch their own businesses, with all the risks and time commitments that that entails.

But the Baby Boomers are, especially if they are considering pop-ups. They have the time. They have completed many of the financial obligations associated with completing their education, building their careers, and raising a family. They are in many ways newly liberated, with a landscape of opportunities appealing to them to plant seeds and cultivate gardens. In fact, recently the Small Business Administration and the American Association of

Retired Persons announced a joint initiative aimed at supporting the entrepreneurial goals and efforts of the retired community.

Add to that the results of a University of Phoenix survey indicating that 26 percent of those over 60 not already running their own businesses had a desire to do so, even during their retirement years, and you have a group of (almost) fresh-faced artisans, collectors, educators, and experienced workers ready to launch businesses. But not any kind of business—they want to pursue their long-dreamt-about passions and ambitions, but not necessarily on a full-time, "all-in" basis. They want a balance with the freedom they have to enjoy their retirement and opportunities to travel, play, read, and spend time with family and friends.

The obvious answer is pop-ups. As an example, let's take a person who just retired, is about to live on Social Security but is looking for just a bit of additional income to cover expenses. Over his adult life, he has developed an avocation of pickling vegetables such as cucumbers and peppers that he has grown each year in his garden, preserving them and giving them to friends as gifts. Now think of the once-a-week farmers market that is open nearby from June through September. What a great opportunity for this Baby Boomer! A chance to continue his love for gardening, to capitalize on a hobby that he has perfected, and the opportunity to make money without having to commit more than one morning a week. This is truly a perfect situation.

This scenario is presenting itself more and more. People who are naturally gifted artists have an opportunity to immerse themselves in an area in which their talents lie. Artists can hone their craft, taking time to learn techniques and to take the time to bring their talents to their highest levels. Then, rather than simply sitting back and admiring their own accomplishments, they can take part in open artist studios and art fairs to promote and actually sell their art.

Also contributing to this changing commercial setting is the Internet, which offers e-commerce and social media platforms. Seniors can join existing networks such as Etsy, eBay, and Shopify, to name a few, and start selling their handmade or collected merchandise online. Those who want to provide a service rather than a portfolio of products, such as those who are great cooks or have skills to teach, can now create pop-ups and promote them through such social networks as Facebook, Twitter, Pinterest, and others. If they need to improve their social media skills, they have the time to sharpen their abilities via continuing education courses and, yes, pop-up classes.

It is often said that the older generation has so much to offer. At the same time, there were not enough channels available for them to showcase what they have learned and can give (or sell). Pop-ups are a new outlet not only for artisans and craftspeople at large, but they are particularly relevant for Baby Boomers as they enter into a new phase of their lives.

About the Author

Jeremy Baras is the founder and C.E.O. of PopUp Republic, an online marketing company that promotes and executes pop-up shops, pop-up restaurants, pop-up events, and pop-up spaces throughout North America. Through its online directory, PopUp Republic provides a forum in which pop-up organizers can promote their events. The company has also executed pop-up concepts for several prominent national brands. Prior to his experience as an entrepreneur, Jeremy worked in sports for the Boston Red Sox. He holds a BA in community entrepreneurship from the University of Vermont. Jeremy can be reached at jbaras@popuprepublic.com.

Index

Page references followed by *p* indicate a photograph.